40 DEVOTIONS FOR TEENAGERS

Reframing

Jesus

A FRESH LOOK INTO A FAMILIAR FACE

simply for students

RICK LAWRENCE AND KURT JOHNSTON

ILLUSTRATION BY STORM

YouthMinistry.com/TOGETHER

Reframing Jesus
A Fresh Look Into a Familiar Face

© 2014 Rick Lawrence, Kurt Johnston, and Jeff A. Storm

group.com
simplyyouthministry.com

CREDITS

Authors: Rick Lawrence and Kurt Johnston
Illustration: Jeff A. Storm
Chief Creative Officer: Joani Schultz
Editor: Rob Cunningham
Cover Art: Jeff A. Storm and Veronica Preston
Project Manager: Stephanie Krajec

Unless otherwise noted, Scripture quotations are taken from the *New American
Standard Bible®*. Copyright © 1960, 1962, 1963, 1968, 1971, 1972, 1973, 1975, 1977,
1995 by The Lockman Foundation. Used by permission. All rights reserved.

Scripture quotations marked (NIV) are taken from the Holy Bible, New International Version®,
NIV®. Copyright © 1973, 1978, 1984, 2011 by Biblica, Inc.™ Used by permission of Zondervan. All
rights reserved worldwide. www.zondervan.com The "NIV" and "New International Version"
are trademarks registered in the United States Patent and Trademark Office by Biblica, Inc.™

Scripture quotations marked THE MESSAGE from *THE MESSAGE*.
Copyright © by Eugene H. Peterson 1993, 1994, 1995, 1996, 2000, 2001,
2002. Used by permission of NavPress Publishing Group.

ISBN: 978-1-4707-2071-1

10 9 8 7 6 5 4 3 2 1   20 19 18 17 16 15 14

Printed in the U.S.A.

CONTENTS

Reframing Jesus

A FRESH LOOK INTO A FAMILIAR FACE

For more than two millennia, Jesus has been at the center of pretty much everything. No one has had a bigger influence on your daily life than Jesus, whether or not that's obvious to you.

Did you know...

- Until Jesus, most human beings were slaves, condemned to perpetual hard labor and captive to the whims of their owners. Jesus upended that system of slavery...

- Until Jesus, women had no rights whatsoever in society. Jesus gave women dignity and status...

- Until Jesus, many pagan religions tried to "appease the gods" with human sacrifice—often children were the most popular sacrifices. Jesus elevated children as treasures to be nurtured...

- Until Jesus, each culture and society determined the passage of time differently—many created "calendars" based on

when the current monarch assumed his office. Because of Jesus, all of human history is organized around his birth and death—it either happened before him or after him...

- Until Jesus, becoming a "learned person" was a goal reserved only for the rich and elite. Jesus called everybody, no matter their social status, to love God "with our whole mind," and institutions of higher learning and libraries sprang up as a result...

- Until Jesus, the most common form of government was totalitarian and despotic. Jesus stripped rulers of their self-proclaimed deity, paving the way for common law and limited government...

- Until Jesus, the sick, infirm, and disabled were considered disposable. Because Jesus emphasized the dignity of the person and elevated the plight of the poor, mercy for those who are hurting became a societal norm, leading to the building of hospitals and social service organizations...

- Until Jesus, forgiveness was a disgusting sign of weakness. Jesus told us to forgive "seventy times seven," and made the love of our enemies the marker for true love...

Yale historian Jaroslav Pelikan says this: "Regardless of what anyone may personally think or believe about him, Jesus of Nazareth has been the dominant figure in the history of Western Culture for almost twenty centuries. If it were possible, with some sort of super magnet, to pull up out of the history every scrap of metal bearing at least a trace of his name, how much would be left?"

Everything seems to orbit around the things Jesus said and did. So you'd think that someone whose influence is so widespread, whose name is so well-known, and whose impact is so lasting would be the most *understood* person in the world.

But he's not.

Most of us think we have a pretty good handle on who Jesus is and what he did. But we don't. He's the most-known, least-known person in history. It's like this—sometimes the people we know the least are the people we're around the most. We take for granted that we know who they really are, because they've always been part of the wallpaper of our life. So we need to be re-introduced to the people and things we think we already know, because we don't really know them as well as we think we do.

And that's the point of this book—to "reframe" what you think you already know about Jesus, so you can grow in your relationship with him. The three of us are no different than you in this—we're very aware of how much we've "missed" who Jesus really is, and we're hungry to know him better.

Thanks for going on this journey with us... We believe it will change your life the way it's changed our lives...

KURT JOHNSTON, RICK LAWRENCE, AND STORM

An Acronym Gone Bad

Ever heard of the "What Would Jesus Do?" movement? Some years ago it was really big—the central question people were asking themselves was simple: "If Christians are supposed to be following Jesus, why aren't they making more of an impact in their daily lives?" The movement's answer was to imagine what everyday life might be like if all of us simply talked and acted more like Jesus. Well, that would change everything—especially if we took a Taco Bell burrito, blessed it, and fed a stadium full of people with it. But, by any measure, the WWJD movement didn't change everything.

Maybe the "Christian" lives we think we're living are actually disconnected from who Jesus really is. It's fine to imagine what we think Jesus might do when a friend betrays us or the test comes back with a "D" on it or we break our finger in a fluke accident right before the big game, but really the whole thing desperately depends on how well we really know the true Jesus, doesn't it? Here's something profound: We can miss Jesus entirely by arrogantly assuming that our imagined responses to a partially understood Jesus mean that we're really following Jesus.

Q: IN ONE SENTENCE, WHAT DOES "FOLLOWING JESUS" MEAN TO YOU, ANYWAY?

RE-FRAME-ABLE

QUICK, GO FIND A PENCIL... WE'LL WAIT FOR YOU TO GET BACK.

SINCE THIS LITTLE BOOK IS ALL ABOUT REFRAMING JESUS, IT'S A GOOD IDEA TO DISCOVER HOW YOU CURRENTLY FRAME HIM—HOW YOU VIEW HIM, IMAGINE HIM, AND DESCRIBE HIM.

IN THE FRAME ABOVE, WRITE DOWN A BUNCH OF STUFF ABOUT JESUS; ANYTHING YOU WANT. ONE-WORD DESCRIPTIONS, THINGS YOU KNOW HE SAID, MIRACLES HE PERFORMED, WHATEVER COMES TO MIND. FILL THAT THING UP, AS QUICKLY AS YOU CAN. YOU MIGHT EVEN WANT TO WRITE YOUR ANSWER TO TODAY'S QUESTION, "WHAT DOES FOLLOWING JESUS MEAN TO YOU?"

AS YOU WORK THROUGH THIS BOOK, COME BACK TO THIS FIRST EXERCISE FROM TIME TO TIME TO SEE HOW YOUR PICTURE OF JESUS IS CHANGING, MATURING, MORPHING, AND, BEST OF ALL, HOW IT'S BEGINNING TO CHANGE YOU ALONG THE WAY!

Why All the

We'd like to apologize for something we're pretty sure has happened to you—somewhere along the way, someone in a church has probably told you that you *should* love Jesus because, well, you're *supposed to*...Jesus doesn't want a "supposed-to" relationship with us; he wants to be known and loved for who he is—and the only way that's going to happen is for us to slow down and get to know his heart.

Have we really soaked in the personality of Jesus—pursued him as the most fascinating, magnetic, lightning-bolt person who ever lived? And if he's really all that incredible, why are "supposed-to's" even necessary? People who are caught up in a romantic relationship don't have to be told to focus on the person of their affection; it's hard to stop thinking about them, actually. No matter what we're doing or who we're with, our thoughts stray to the object of our passion. And that's not because we "should" be zoned in on the object of our affection—we simply can't help ourselves, because we're mesmerized by so much beauty. Jesus wants to capture our hearts, not force our obedience.

OK, NOW HERE'S A LITTLE THOUGHT FOR THE DAY: HOW DO YOU THINK PEOPLE IN YOUR LIFE (PARENTS, SIBLINGS, FRIENDS, TEACHERS, STRANGERS) WOULD BE AFFECTED IF THE JESUS-IN-YOU WAS GIVEN GREATER FREEDOM TO LIVE OUT, IN YOUR EVERYDAY LIFE, SOME OF THE SAME QUALITIES THAT YOU FIND SO ATTRACTIVE IN HIM?

'Shoulds'?

IF YOU'RE READING THIS BOOK, WE'RE GUESSING YOU'D LIKELY SAY THAT YOU LOVE JESUS. BUT WHY? HOPEFULLY, IT'S NOT SIMPLY BECAUSE YOU FEEL LIKE YOU SHOULD-LIKE YOU'RE SUPPOSED TO! SO WHAT IS IT ABOUT JESUS THAT HAS DRAWN YOU TO HIM; WHAT ABOUT HIM HAS MADE YOU WANT TO LOVE HIM? NEVER REALLY THOUGHT ABOUT THAT? THAT'S OK; MOST PEOPLE HAVEN'T. SO HERE'S YOUR CHANCE! THERE'S SOME ← SPACE TO JOT DOWN SOME OF THE THINGS YOU LOVE ABOUT JESUS-THINGS ABOUT HIM THAT HAVE DRAWN YOU TOWARD HIM, NOT BECAUSE YOU SHOULD, BUT BECAUSE YOU WANT TO!

What's the Big Deal

Hey, if we call ourselves Christians, that means Jesus is a big deal to us, right? Well, for a lot of us who identify as Christians, Jesus isn't **really** at the center of our orbit. We like to think he is, but if we're honest, other pursuits in our life are often a lot more important to us than the pursuit of Jesus. It'd be super-hard to admit that we've sidelined Jesus, but our actions are drowning out our words—we have so many other must-do's and must-have's and must-be's pressuring us. It's not like we're the first to get lured into this trap...

Incredible as it sounds, the thousands of people who were following Jesus all left him when Jesus upped the ante for them...he'd just told them that they'd need to "eat the flesh of the Son of Man and drink His blood" if they wanted to follow

RE-FRAME-ABLE FOR PETER, AND MOST OF THE EARLY FOLLOWERS OF JESUS, FOLLOWING JESUS WAS SOMETIMES SCARY, OFTEN CONFUSING, AND OCCASIONALLY PAINFUL! IT WASN'T EASY, BUT IT WAS SO WORTH IT!

THERE'S PROBABLY BEEN STUFF IN YOUR LIFE THAT WASN'T EASY, BUT WAS SO WORTH IT!

- GETTING GOOD GRADES—NOT EASY, BUT SO WORTH IT!
- TRYING OUT FOR A SCHOOL PLAY OR SPORTS TEAM—NOT EASY, BUT SO WORTH IT!
- BREAKING A BAD HABIT—NOT EASY, BUT SO WORTH IT!
- CHOOSING NOT TO PUNCH YOUR LITTLE BROTHER—NOT EASY, BUT SO WORTH IT!

About Jesus?

him (John 6:53). That freaks them out, so they abandon him. And Jesus asks his remaining disciples this vulnerable question: "You do not want to go away also, do you?" (v. 67). Peter responds with this equally vulnerable declaration: "Lord, to whom shall we go? You have words of eternal life. We have believed and have come to know that You are the Holy One of God" (v. 68-69). In effect, he's saying: "I don't know what 'eat my body and drink my blood' really means, and a lot of what you do and say is a mystery to me, but you've ruined me for you." The ultimate reason we put other things, instead of Jesus, at the center of our life is that we can. We're not yet "ruined" for him.

YET MANY CONTEMPORARY FOLLOWERS OF JESUS HAVE PAINTED A PICTURE THAT FOLLOWING HIM IS SUPPOSED TO BE EASY, FUN, AND FULL OF SUNSHINE. MAYBE YOU NEED TO REFRAME JESUS? MAYBE FOLLOWING HIM IS, IN SOME WAYS, MORE LIKE A BUNCH OF OTHER STUFF IN YOUR LIFE-NOT EASY, BUT SO WORTH IT!

HERE'S AN IDEA! JOT DOWN YOUR TOP "NOT EASY" PART OF BEING A TEENAGER WHO IS TRYING TO FOLLOW JESUS. THEN, UNDER IT, WRITE DOWN WHY, EVEN THOUGH IT'S NOT EASY, IT'S "SO WORTH IT!"

why it's so worth it →

The Disappearing Jesus

A junior high girl had just served as a leader in a churchwide worship experience during Holy Week. She'd spent several days leading people from her congregation into a deeper relationship with Jesus through an interactive devotional experience. In the midst of her giddy excitement about the experience, she was asked to describe Jesus. She scrunched her forehead, then offered this hopeful response: "Well, I'd have to say he's really, really nice."

Well, what about the time Jesus made a whip and chased all the money-changers out of the Temple? The girl scrunched her forehead again, and the smile disappeared from her face. Finally, she blurted: "Well, I know Jesus is nice, so what he did must have been nice." Her response represents the norm in our culture—most people, no matter how old, primarily describe Jesus as "nice." And that's profoundly sad. Why? Well, of course, Jesus was "nice" to the people he healed or fed or rescued. But he would never be voted Mr. Congeniality. He definitely wasn't nice when he was blasting (over and over) religious leaders or calling his lead disciple "Satan" or an innocent Canaanite woman a "dog."

The point is that a *merely* nice Jesus is no Jesus at all; he's like a declawed version of Narnia's Aslan. And if the Jesus we know isn't really the Jesus of the Bible, our passion for him will grow weak. We crave a real relationship with a real person.

RE-FRAME-ABLE

PART OF THE PROCESS OF REFRAMING JESUS IS THE
WILLINGNESS TO THINK ABOUT HIM DIFFERENTLY, TO SEE HIM
IN NEW WAYS. PERHAPS THE IDEA THAT JESUS WASN'T ALWAYS
MR. NICE GUY IS A BRAND-NEW THOUGHT TO YOU. HOORAY!
YOU'RE ON YOUR WAY TO REFRAMING JESUS! SO LET'S KEEP
THINKING ABOUT THIS IDEA. HERE ARE A FEW QUESTIONS TO
GET YOU STARTED:

- JESUS WASN'T ALWAYS "NICE," BUT HE WAS ALWAYS
  MOTIVATED BY LOVE. HOW CAN THAT BE POSSIBLE?

- CAN YOU THINK OF A TIME WHEN YOU WERE OVERLY
  CONCERNED ABOUT BEING "NICE"-MAYBE TO THE POINT
  THAT IT ACTUALLY DID MORE HARM THAN GOOD?

- HERE'S A TOUGH ONE: JESUS WASN'T ALWAYS "NICE," BUT
  THE BIBLE TEACHES THAT HIS SPIRIT LIVING IN US WANTS
  TO PRODUCE KINDNESS IN US (GALATIANS 5:22-23). WHAT
  ARE WE SUPPOSED TO DO WITH THAT?

SOMETIMES THERE ARE NO EASY ANSWERS. LIKE WE
DISCOVERED IN THE LAST CHAPTER, SOME OF THIS REFRAMING
JESUS STUFF IS NOT EASY-BUT IT'S SO WORTH IT!

Be the Pig

Don't expect to drop your underwear off at the French Laundry in Napa Valley—it's actually one of the world's top-rated restaurants. And if you're a waiter or a dishwasher or a shift manager or a sous chef, the highest honor you can earn is the coveted "Be the Pig" T-shirt, given only to the best of the best who work there. The slogan refers to the difference between pigs and chickens. A chicken might offer up an egg for the meal, but the pig gives his life for it.

People who have been "ruined" for Jesus are pigs, not chickens.

So, how do we move from chicken to pig? Well, when we so identify ourselves with Jesus that we can't imagine leaving him, then we're pigs.

Paul, an all-in disciple and one of the greatest thinkers in history, describes his orientation to Jesus this way: "I resolved to know nothing while I was with you except Jesus Christ and him crucified" (1 Corinthians 2:2, NIV). What does he mean by "know nothing" anyway? He's using hyperbole to emphasize his priority—to spend his energy and his passion and his intellect to know Jesus, with pig-like determination. He's not interested in facts and trivia and "right answers" about Jesus. Paul wants to know Jesus the way you know your best friend—inside-out. He wants to know him so well that he can finish Jesus' sentences. That's living a pig's life...

RE-FRAME-ABLE CHECK OUT THIS LIST...

_____ FRIENDS	_____ FITTING IN
_____ FAMILY	_____ CHOIR
_____ SPORTS	_____ DRAMA
_____ SCHOOL	_____ DANCE
_____ HANGING OUT ONLINE	_____ BAND
_____ BEING POPULAR	_____ DEBATE
_____ FIGURING OUT HOW TO	_____ YOUR JOB
GET THE STUFF YOU WANT	_____ YOUR BOYFRIEND/GIRLFRIEND

OK, NOW IT'S TIME FOR A "PIG CHECK"! FROM OUR LIST, CHOOSE THE ONES THAT YOU SPEND AT LEAST A LITTLE OF YOUR TIME ON, AND NEXT TO EACH ONE WRITE PIG (SOMETHING YOU'RE SERIOUSLY INVESTED IN) OR CHICKEN (SOMETHING YOU'RE ONLY MARGINALLY INVESTED IN).

-IF YOU WANT TO LIVE A "PIG'S LIFE" FOR JESUS, WHAT ARE YOUR CHIEF COMPETITORS IN LIFE?

-WHAT MAKES SOME THINGS IN OUR LIFE WORTHY OF "PIG-LEVEL" COMMITMENT, AND OTHERS NOT?

GUEST CHECK

DATE	SERVER	TABLE	QUESTS	CHECK NUMBER
				689561

→ IN THE END, THERE WERE NO CHICKENS AMONG JESUS' 12 DISCIPLES—THEY ALL GAVE THEIR LIVES FOR HIM. RELATIVE TO JESUS, WHERE ARE YOU ON THE CHICKEN-TO-PIG CONTINUUM?

The Real Thing

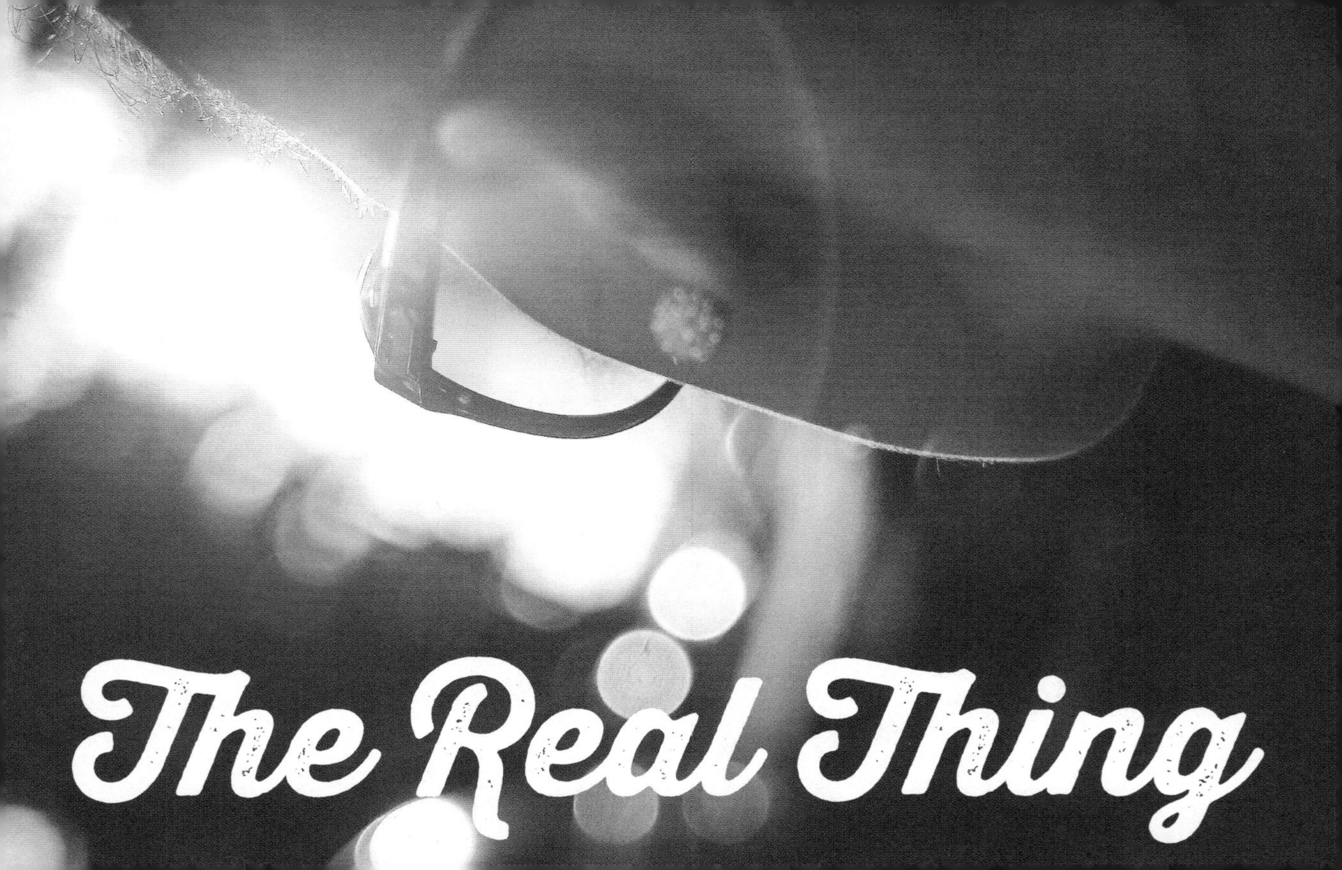

N.T. Wright is the most prolific biblical scholar of our time—many consider the retired Anglican bishop the "heir apparent" to the great C.S. Lewis. And Wright says this about the magnetic pull Jesus has on those who will pull off the highway of their life long enough to study him: "The longer you look at Jesus, the more you will want to serve him. That is, of course, if it's the real Jesus you're looking at."

It's "the real Jesus" whose gravitational pull is so strong that we can't escape his orbit once we get close to him. But "the real Jesus" implies that there's also a "fake Jesus" out there. Philosophy professor and C.S. Lewis scholar Dr. Peter Kreeft once told a class of Boston University students:

"Christ changed every human being he ever met.... If anyone claims to have met him without being changed, he has not met him at all. When you touch him, you touch lightning.... I think Jesus is the only man in history who never bored anyone. The Greek word used to describe everyone's reaction to him in the Gospels is 'thauma'—wonder. This was true of his enemies, who killed him. Of his disciples, who worshipped him. And even of agnostics, who went away shaking their heads and muttering 'No man every spoke like this man' and knowing that if he didn't stop being what he was and saying what he said that eventually they would have to side with either his killers or his worshippers..."

Our life isn't really about learning all the right answers—it's about encountering the real Jesus, who will change our lives...

RE-FRAME-ABLE

TURN BACK TO THE VERY FIRST CHAPTER OF THIS BOOK. THERE, YOU JOTTED DOWN SOME OF THE STUFF YOU KNOW ABOUT JESUS. NOW IT'S TIME TO ADD TO THE LIST-WRITE DOWN ONE OR TWO THINGS ABOUT JESUS THAT TRULY CAUSE YOU TO RESPOND WITH AWE... WITH WONDER. YOU KNOW, MIND-BLOWING STUFF ABOUT JESUS.

IF IT'S TRUE THAT EVERYBODY WHO EVER MET JESUS HAS BEEN CHANGED, IT SHOULD BE PRETTY EASY TO THINK ABOUT HOW HE HAS IMPACTED YOUR LIFE. IN THE SPACE BELOW, WRITE TWO THINGS.

1. WHAT'S ONE WAY JESUS HAS TRULY CHANGED YOUR LIFE?

2. HOW HAS THIS IMPACTED THE WAY YOU LIVE YOUR DAY-TO-DAY LIFE?

Attachment Trumps Talent

What kinds of people change the world? Well, we assume it's the really smart ones—the highly talented, most widely connected, best-educated, and most-driven people who have what it takes. From Steve Jobs to Bill Gates to Mark Zuckerberg to Michael Jordan to Desmond Tutu, world-changing people always have some kind of transcendent ability that's a difference-maker.

So how do we explain the ragtag group of nobodies Jesus chose as his closest disciples and confidants—the mostly uneducated, blue-collar grunts who ended up changing the world so profoundly that everyone everywhere is impacted by what they did? The simple reason these often-clueless first-century men and women upended the world is because their "movement" was attached to the present force of the person of Jesus. They weren't the greatest tips-and-techniques people who ever walked the earth. They weren't skilled at strategy or structure. But they were ruined for Jesus, and that attachment changed everything they touched.

In his book *Who Is This Man?* author and pastor John Ortberg sums it up well: "Normally when someone dies, their impact on the world immediately begins to recede. ... Jesus' impact was greater a hundred years after his death than during his life; it was greater still after five hundred years; after a thousand years his legacy laid the foundation for much of Europe; after two thousand years he has more followers in more places than ever."

Real impact in the world isn't ultimately tied to our gifts and abilities; it's tied to his gifts and abilities empowering us to move mountains...

THAT'S SOME STUFF WORTH THINKING ABOUT.

QUESTION #1: WHAT ARE SOME OF THE THINGS YOU ARE REALLY GOOD AT? AND HAVE YOU EVER THOUGHT ABOUT THE "ELEPHANT IN THE LIVING ROOM"—THAT JESUS GAVE YOU YOUR ABILITIES AND TALENTS? THAT'S THE REASON YOU LOVE THE THINGS YOU LOVE—HE'S WIRED YOU THAT WAY FROM THE VERY BEGINNING...

QUESTION #2: DID YOU KNOW THAT JESUS IS STILL IN THE BUSINESS OF LOOKING FOR YOUNG MEN AND WOMEN WHO ARE WILLING TO GO "ALL IN" FOR HIM, JUST AS THE ORIGINAL DISCIPLES DID?

QUESTION #3: HAVE YOU EVER THOUGHT ABOUT WHAT A DIFFERENCE YOU COULD MAKE IN THE LIVES OF PEOPLE AROUND YOU, AND MAYBE EVEN THE WORLD, IF YOU SPENT YOUR LIFE DOING SOMETHING YOU LOVE AND YOU'RE GOOD AT, TREATING IT AS YOUR "SPIRITUAL SERVICE OF WORSHIP" (ROMANS 12:1)? IT'S AN ATTITUDE THAT SAYS: "JESUS, I'M ALL IN! YOU WIRED ME THE WAY YOU DID SO I CAN MAKE A LASTING DIFFERENCE IN THE WORLD... LET'S DO THIS THING!"

RE-FRAME-ABLE

MOTHER TERESA

Paying Ridiculous Attention

The Incredulity of Saint Thomas (Caravaggio)

RE-FRAME-ABLE

IN THE VERY FIRST CHAPTER, YOU
WROTE DOWN SOME THINGS YOU
THINK YOU KNOW ABOUT JESUS.
NOW, WRITE DOWN THREE THINGS
YOU KNOW YOU KNOW ABOUT
JESUS-STUFF THAT YOU ARE CERTAIN
ABOUT...

1.

2.

3.

WHAT DO THESE THINGS TEACH YOU
ABOUT GOD? AND-THIS IS WHERE
IT GETS A LITTLE BIT CHALLENGING-
HOW DO THESE TRUTHS ABOUT GOD
IMPACT THE WAY YOU LIVE YOUR LIFE
AND RELATE TO THE PEOPLE GOD
PUTS IN YOUR PATH?

In his book *Ruthless Trust*, author Brennan Manning writes: "It must be noted that Jesus alone reveals who God is. ... We cannot deduce anything about Jesus from what we think we know about God; however, we must deduce everything about God from what we know about Jesus." This is... Just. So. True. Our misconceptions about God won't help us understand Jesus. But studying Jesus will very much help us understand God. Maybe our biggest question in life is this: "Is there a God, and if so, what is that God like?" Manning is suggesting the best way to answer that question is to pay ridiculous attention to everything Jesus said and did. We learn "everything about God" by slowing way down to consider what Jesus actually said, whom he actually said it to, and what actual impact his words and actions had on people.

When we let our determined pursuit of Jesus guide our understanding of God, our life will be transformed by what we discover. For example, if Jesus is a mirror for God's *exact* character and personality, what do we know about God's attitude toward sin based on the way Jesus responded to the "sinner" woman who crashed a high-society part and washed his feet with her tears and hair (Luke 7)? A Pharisee, host of the party, was appalled by this disgusting behavior, and wondered how Jesus could tolerate this "sort of person." But Jesus told him that people who love much are forgiven much.

There is no longing in our hearts that can't be satisfied by "eating and drinking" more of Jesus. But the first thing we must do: We must remember the Jesus we didn't know we'd forgotten.

From Knowing About to Knowing

Sometimes we pray in silence—kind of a "date" conversation with Jesus, where it's just "you and me." And sometimes we pray out loud, so others can hear. This is more like a "group date," where it's "you and us." In his High Priestly Prayer (John 17), Jesus tells his Father out loud, with his disciples gathered near, that he's accomplished everything he's been given to do, and that things are about to get better for them because he's about to leave. Why is he praying out loud, and why would he speak so positively about leaving his followers?

We'd rather be with the people we love than away from them. But here Jesus almost can't wait to leave, because that means the people he loves will "get" him more fully than they have so far. He wants them (and us) to know that our longing to know him more deeply can only happen if he "hands the baton" to the Holy Spirit. On the road to Emmaus two of his disciples prove that much of what the Good Shepherd Jesus tried to get across to his sheep hadn't really "stuck." They'd heard him, lived with him, and watched him, but they hadn't yet been transformed by him. One crucial step was left: to move from an *outside* influence to an *inside* influence. And that's why the Holy Spirit is so necessary. The Spirit makes it possible for us to move from *knowing about* Jesus to *knowing* Jesus. This is *knowing* in the "biblical sense"—it's our most intimate act.

RE-FRAME-ABLE

THIS IS AN EASY LITTLE ADVENTURE, BUT ONE YOU'LL LIKELY FORGET TO DO UNLESS YOU DO SOMETHING DRASTIC. WE'LL GIVE YOU SOME IDEAS ABOUT THAT IN A SECOND, BUT FIRST THE "ADVENTURE."

IF YOU'RE READING THIS BOOK, YOU LIKELY HAVE SOME CONNECTION TO A CHURCH (GOOD FOR YOU-GIVE YOURSELF A LITTLE GOLF CLAP). CHANCES ARE, EVERY TIME YOU GO TO YOUTH GROUP YOU LEARN ABOUT GOD, JESUS, AND THE BIBLE. SO, JUST FOR THE NEXT MONTH, APPROACH YOUTH GROUP A LITTLE DIFFERENTLY. NO MATTER WHAT YOU'RE LEARNING ABOUT, ASK JESUS TO HELP YOU USE THAT INFORMATION TO ACTUALLY KNOW HIM BETTER.

LEARNING ABOUT THE TEN COMMANDMENTS? HOW CAN YOU KNOW JESUS BETTER AS A RESULT?

LEARNING ABOUT PEER PRESSURE? HOW CAN YOU KNOW JESUS BETTER AS A RESULT?

SO YOU DON'T FORGET TO DO THIS, DO SOMETHING DRASTIC TO REMIND YOURSELF. HERE ARE A FEW IDEAS:

- WRITE "KNOW JESUS" ON YOUR BATHROOM MIRROR USING A BAR OF SOAP.

- ASK YOUR MOM TO SEND YOU A TEXT MESSAGE WHILE YOU'RE AT YOUTH GROUP THAT SIMPLY SAYS, "KNOW JESUS."

- WRITE "KNOW JESUS" ON A PIECE OF MASKING TAPE AND ASK YOUR SMALL GROUP LEADER TO WEAR IT ON HIS/HER FOREHEAD DURING BIBLE STUDY SO YOU'LL REMEMBER THAT WHATEVER HE/SHE IS TEACHING ABOUT, IT'S ULTIMATELY ABOUT KNOWING JESUS!

Jesus repeatedly described the people of God as sheep, and for good reason. Sheep are not exactly quick of mind, if you know what I mean. They're...

- Timid, fearful, and easily panicked...
- Typically stupid and gullible...
- Vulnerable to fear, frustration, pests, and hunger...
- Easily influenced by a strong, calm leader...
- Easily prodded into a stampede—they're vulnerable to a "mob mentality"...
- Have little or no means of self-defense, and are easily killed by their enemies...
- Jealous and competitive for dominance...
- Always seeking fresh water and fresh pastures, but aren't very discerning in their choices...
- Stubborn and always insisting on their own way...
- Easily tipped over onto their back, and are unable to right themselves...
- Bothered by someone who tries to clean or shear their wool...
- Creatures of habit that often get stuck in "ruts"...
- Needy—they require more care than any other livestock...

It's hard to write all this, knowing that Jesus compares me to this embarrassing animal—in fact, it's pretty easy to see myself in a lot of these bullet points. But here's an overarching truth about Jesus' relationship with sheep: "When [Jesus] saw the crowds, he had compassion on them, because they were harassed and helpless, like sheep without a shepherd" (Matthew 9:36–37, NIV). The deepest truth is summed up in a well-known lyric from a children's song: "Jesus loves us, this I know..." He wants to Shepherd us because he loves us. Sheep don't need a better understanding of how to avoid getting eaten by wolves; we need a deeper trust in and obedience to our fierce Shepherd, who will look out for us, defend us, and rescue us.

Sheep-i-ness

RE-FRAME-ABLE

{ QUESTION: WHAT ARE SOME AREAS THAT YOU ARE TRYING TO NAVIGATE ALL ON YOUR OWN (TRYING TO BE INDEPENDENT) THAT YOU SHOULD ASK THE GOOD SHEPHERD FOR SOME HELP (DEPENDENT)? }

Remembering

TO REMEMBER

If remembering Jesus is central to our spiritual growth and our impact in the world, then forgetting is our greatest enemy. And that's a problem, because most of us are way, way too comfortable and satisfied in our knowledge and understanding and experience of Jesus. That's why discomfort is such a great way to leverage our remembering. Pain has the power to expose our determination to live our lives independent from Jesus—as long as we have everything under control ourselves, we're not that interested in depending on our Good Shepherd. The more on top of things the sheep think they are, the more exposed they are to danger, because they'll be less interested in listening to and obeying their Shepherd and more committed to fighting their own (impossible-to-win) battles.

The Apostle Paul, in his old age and with the end of his life on the horizon, gave his protégé Timothy this bit of parting advice: "Remember Jesus Christ, raised from the dead, descended from David. This is my gospel, for which I am suffering even to the point of being chained like a criminal" (2 Timothy 2:8-9, NIV). Paul was imprisoned because of his aggressive pursuit of Jesus, and Timothy had lived through beatings and shipwrecks and imprisonments with him—all for the glory and honor of Jesus. Why would Paul have to remind Timothy about Jesus? Because he was humble enough to admit the truth: Everyone, including Paul, Timothy, John the Baptist, Peter, and the disciples...and now you and me...is a notorious forgetter. Never assume the Jesus you think you know is the Jesus of reality—when you "eat or drink" him, you'll quickly blast away your false assumptions...

RE-FRAME-ABLE

HUMANS ARE GREAT AT FORGETTING (UNLESS YOUR PARENTS OWE YOU MONEY, THEN YOU NEVER FORGET). JESUS KNEW THIS—WHICH IS WHY, BEFORE HE PHYSICALLY LEFT THE EARTH, HE HAD A MASSIVE BANQUET WITH HIS FOLLOWERS WHERE THEY ATE TASTY FOOD AND DRANK WINE TOGETHER TO REMEMBER WHAT JESUS' MISSION ON EARTH WAS ALL ABOUT. THE CHURCH YOU ATTEND PROBABLY PARTICIPATES IN A SIMPLE, BUT IMPORTANT, VERSION OF THIS EVENT THAT TODAY IS USUALLY CALLED COMMUNION OR THE LORD'S SUPPER. THE SIMPLE ACT OF TAKING COMMUNION IS MEANT TO BE A VERY POWERFUL REMINDER OF THE POWER OF JESUS' LIFE, DEATH, AND RESURRECTION. WE ARE SHEEP. WE ARE GOOD AT FORGETTING. SOME PEOPLE TIE A STRING ON THEIR FINGER AS A REMINDER OF SOMETHING IMPORTANT.

WHAT'S SOMETHING YOU CAN WEAR, OR PIN TO YOUR BACKPACK, OR WRITE ON YOUR HAND, THAT WILL HELP YOU REMEMBER HOW BADLY YOU NEED THE GOOD SHEPHERD—TODAY AND EVERY DAY?

Why All This Useless Beauty?

There are almost 9 million separate species in the world (8.74 million, to be exact). And thousands of new species are discovered every year. Researchers estimate it will still take hundreds of years for human beings, with all our cleverness, to discover them all. To quote a great Elvis Costello song, "Why all this useless beauty"? The answer is that God's "love language" is the language of metaphor. According to Romans 1:20, God has buried clues to his true nature in… nature: "Since the creation of the world his invisible attributes, His eternal power and divine nature, have been clearly seen, being understood through what has been made." Every created thing is actually a metaphor—something that's symbolic of something else—that can help us understand who God really is and what he's really like.

Jesus used this same strategy to help us understand how spiritual growth works: "I am the Vine, you are the branches. When you're joined with me and I with you, the relation intimate and organic, the harvest is sure to be abundant. Separated, you can't produce a thing. Anyone who separates from me is deadwood, gathered up and thrown on the bonfire" (John 15:5-6, THE MESSAGE).

This joined-to-the-Vine metaphor is telling us a deep truth—we're just dying branches in desperate need of attaching ourselves to a growing Vine, and the Vine is Jesus himself.

DID JESUS REALLY SAY THAT WHEN WE'RE DETACHED FROM HIM, WE CAN'T PRODUCE ANYTHING? REALLY JESUS? YEP, HE SAID IT AND HE REALLY MEANT IT. THINK ABOUT IT—A BRANCH SEPARATED FROM THE REST OF THE PLANT IS STILL A BRANCH... IT'S JUST NOT A VERY EFFECTIVE BRANCH. IT'S NOT DOING WHAT BRANCHES ARE ULTIMATELY SUPPOSED TO DO. AND WHAT ARE BRANCHES ULTIMATELY SUPPOSED TO DO? THEY'RE SUPPOSED TO GROW, BLOSSOM, AND PRODUCE FRUIT. A BRANCH DISCONNECTED FROM THE VINE IS STILL A BRANCH, BUT IT'S KINDA USELESS.

SO JESUS IS MAKING A PRETTY BOLD STATEMENT. HE'S SAYING THAT WHEN WE ARE DISCONNECTED FROM HIM WE AREN'T GROWING, BLOOMING, OR PRODUCING FRUIT—WE'RE KINDA USELESS. OUCH.

PRAYING AND READING THE BIBLE ARE OBVIOUS WAYS WE CAN STAY CONNECTED TO JESUS, SO I JUST GAVE YOU THOSE TWO IDEAS AS FREEBIES! WHAT ARE TWO OR THREE OTHER WAYS YOU CAN STAY CONNECTED TO JESUS, THE VINE, ALL THE TIME?

Following the Beeline

A little over 150 years ago, he was the most famous person in all the world, but you've likely never heard of him. He's C.H. Spurgeon, and he earned the nickname "the prince of preachers" when he was just 22 because of his inspiring sermons as the pastor of London's famous downtown church, New Park Street Chapel. Every Sunday he'd preach twice, to congregations of 6,000 people, before the days of microphones and amplification. Today, he still has more books in print than any pastor in history, including more than 2,500 sermons.

Spurgeon lived by a very simple conviction—to "beeline" everything in his life and ministry to Jesus. Of course, "beeline" is a funny word to us—it means that no matter what he was preaching or teaching about, Spurgeon was always headed to Jesus. Once, a young pastor asked Spurgeon to critique his preaching, and the older man was blunt: "That was a poor sermon." When the young man asked for an explanation, Spurgeon replied: "Because there was no Christ in it." The young man protested that his chosen Scripture verse had nothing to do with Jesus. Spurgeon responded: "Don't you know, young man, that from every town, and every village, and every little hamlet in England, wherever it may be, there is a road to London? And so from *every text* in Scripture there is a road to the metropolis of the Scriptures, that is Christ."

Spurgeon's passion for Jesus, and his determination to track everything he said and did back to "the metropolis of Christ," is the light we need to find our way through a life that can seem like a dark jungle.

ANOTHER WAY TO DEFINE "BEELINE" MIGHT BE: POINTING DIRECTLY TOWARD.

SERMONS ARE AWESOME, AND SPURGEON WAS PRETTY GOOD AT THEM! BUT HERE'S SOMETHING WORTH THINKING ABOUT: THE WAY YOU LIVE YOUR LIFE MAY BE THE MOST IMPORTANT SERMON YOUR FRIENDS WILL EVER HEAR.

IF THAT'S TRUE, AND IF THE BEST SERMONS MAKE A BEELINE (OR POINT DIRECTLY TOWARD) JESUS, THEN MAYBE OUR LIVES NEED TO MAKE A BEELINE (OR POINT DIRECTLY TOWARD) JESUS, TOO! BUT YOU ALREADY KNOW THAT A LOT OF TEENAGERS ARE "POINTING THEIR LIVES" TO ALL SORTS OF STUFF OTHER THAN JESUS...

FOR MANY...

· HOW THEY PICK THEIR FRIENDS POINTS DIRECTLY TOWARD A DESIRE TO BE POPULAR.

· HOW THEY TALK ABOUT OTHERS POINTS DIRECTLY TOWARD A DESIRE TO BELITTLE.

· HOW THEY SPEND THEIR ALONE TIME POINTS DIRECTLY TOWARD A DESIRE TO FEED THEIR OWN SINFUL DESIRES.

THE WAY YOU LIVE YOUR LIFE MAY BE THE MOST IMPORTANT SERMON YOUR FRIENDS WILL EVER HEAR. WHAT IS YOUR SERMON POINTING THEM TO?

RE-FRAME-ABLE

The Truth Itself

As long as we're in the middle of our little Spurgeon-fest, learning what it's like to live a "beelined-to-Jesus" kind of life, let's chew on this from the great preacher: "Jesus is the Truth. We believe in him—not merely in his words. He is... the Revealer and the Revelation, the Illuminator and the Light of Men. He is exalted in every word of truth, because he is its sum and substance... A Christ-less gospel is no gospel at all and a Christ-less discourse is the cause of merriment to devils."

Here's a Victorian-to-Today translation of this—Jesus doesn't merely *point the way* to true things, or *give us an example* of what is true. *He is Truth itself.* So the best way to know Jesus more intimately is to look at him through this filter—whatever he says and does is the very definition of "good and true," because Jesus is the source of everything that is good and true. Chasing the people selling "God-junk" out of the Temple with a whip he created on the spot? Good and true. Calling the religious power-brokers of his day, the Pharisees, offensive names like "whitewashed tombs" and "brood of vipers"? Good and true. Praising a "sinful woman" who crashed a society party and washed his feet with her tears? Good and true.

The more we slow down to consider how Jesus is "good and true," the more we attach ourselves to the "Vine."

RE-FRAME-ABLE

TIME FOR A LITTLE SPIRITUAL, JESUS-Y, EXERCISE! ABOVE, WE LISTED THINGS JESUS SAID OR DID THAT WERE GOOD AND TRUE, EVEN THOUGH NOT EVERYBODY THOUGHT SO AT THE TIME! WE'VE LISTED THEM AGAIN. NEXT TO EACH, WRITE A SENTENCE OR TWO THAT DESCRIBES WHAT (BASED ON WHAT YOU KNOW ABOUT JESUS) MAKES EACH ONE BOTH "GOOD" AND "TRUE".

MAYBE THAT'S A LITTLE TOUGH TO FIGURE OUT, AND THAT'S OK! WE WON'T EVER FULLY UNDERSTAND EVERYTHING ABOUT JESUS, AND THAT'S OK, TOO... ESPECIALLY IF WE UNDERSTAND THAT EVERYTHING ABOUT HIM IS BOTH GOOD AND TRUE.

- CHASING AWAY PEOPLE WHO WERE SELLING THINGS IN THE TEMPLE

- CALLING THE RELIGIOUS LEADERS OUT

- HONORING A SINFUL WOMAN WHO FELL TO HER KNEES TO WORSHIP HIM

A PRAYER FOR TODAY: "JESUS, TODAY WOULD YOU REMIND ME OF YOUR TRUTH AND YOUR GOODNESS. AND AS I STAY CONNECTED TO YOU, THE VINE, PLEASE HELP ME REFLECT YOUR GOODNESS AND TRUTH TO THE WORLD AROUND ME."

The First Question
That Really Matters

What's your life's purpose? The answer to that BIG question is buried, like a priceless treasure, in a remarkable conversation between Jesus and his disciples as they road-tripped through Caesarea Philippi (described in Matthew 16). After another tough encounter with the conniving Pharisees, followed by another frustrating conversation with his confused disciples, Jesus does something shockingly humble. He asks his disciples: "Who do people say that the Son of Man is?" And his nervous disciples throw out: "Some say John the Baptist; and others, Elijah; but still others, Jeremiah, or one of the prophets."

And here's Jesus at his most vulnerable: "But who do you say that I am?"

Have you ever asked your friends, "What do you think of me, really?" If you have, you know it takes guts to ask such an honest question. And it takes even more courage to listen to the response, if it's also honest. In this case, Peter answers: "You are the Christ, the Son of the living God." This is why Peter is such a heroic figure in the Bible—he steps up in an awkward moment and proclaims the truth about who Jesus really is. But the most important thing to pay attention to is Jesus' original question: "Who do you say I am?" This is one of two questions that will lead you to your life's purpose, if you'll pursue it in a new way, every day...

QUESTION

1

RE-FRAME-ABLE

GETTING DECENT GRADES. SEEMS IMPORTANT ENOUGH.

BEING A LOYAL FRIEND. SEEMS IMPORTANT ENOUGH.

GOING TO CHURCH. SEEMS IMPORTANT ENOUGH.

ALWAYS TRYING YOUR BEST. SEEMS IMPORTANT ENOUGH.

IN FACT, ALMOST EVERY ADULT IN YOUR LIFE WOULD BE COMPLETELY OVERJOYED IF YOU EXCELLED AT THOSE FOUR BASIC, FAIRLY IMPORTANT THINGS! AND JESUS WOULD BE OVERJOYED RIGHT ALONGSIDE THEM. BUT HE'S WAY MORE INTERESTED IN HOW YOU WOULD ANSWER THE SAME QUESTION HE ASKED HIS DISCIPLES: "WHO DO YOU SAY THAT I AM?"

PETER GIVES THE PERFECT ANSWER, BUT WHAT DOES IT REALLY MEAN? AND THIS LEADS TO ANOTHER QUESTION:

QUESTION:	What does it really mean to you?	
REFERENCE:	Matthew 18	WHO DO YOU SAY I AM?
ANSWER:		

The Second Question
That Really Matters

When Peter steps up and answers Jesus' question ("Who do you say that I am?") with magnificent determination, he reveals his deepening attachment to Jesus, the "Vine." But close relationships are always a two-way street—so when we consider the truth about who Jesus really is and "name" him, Jesus also considers the truth about who we are and "names" us. After his closest friend is the first to publicly proclaim him as Messiah and the Son of God, Jesus fires back with this: "You are Peter, and upon this rock I will build My church; and the gates of Hades will not overpower it. I will give you the keys of the kingdom of heaven; and whatever you bind on earth shall have been bound in heaven, and whatever you loose on earth shall have been loosed in heaven" (Matthew 16:18-19).

As we have the courage to name Jesus, he is determined to name us, just as he did with Peter. Our purpose in life narrows in focus, simply, to feeding our fascination of all the surprising things Jesus said and did, then staying open to him identifying who we really are and what we're made to do. We move Jesus from the background of our everyday activities into the foreground, and he surfaces our true identity from all the false things we, and others, try to pin on us. The second question that leads us to our life's purpose is simple: **"Who does Jesus say I am?"**

RE-FRAME-ABLE

WRITE YOUR NAME BELOW...

THEN WRITE WHAT YOUR NAME MEANS (YOU CAN GO TO THIS WEBSITE TO FIND THE ORIGIN/
MEANING OF MOST NAMES-BEHINDTHENAME.COM):

THIS IS GONNA FEEL WEIRD, BUT GO WITH IT! PRETEND JESUS WERE TO GIVE YOU A NEW NAME,
A NAME THAT TRULY DESCRIBED HOW HE SEES YOU AND FEELS ABOUT YOU... WRITE DOWN THE
NAME YOU THINK HE'D GIVE YOU, AND WHY. REMEMBER, JESUS IS GOOD AND TRUE, SO HE
WOULD ONLY NAME YOU SOMETHING THAT IS GOOD AND TRUE, TOO!

NAME:	
MEANING:	
NEW NAME:	

Stripped Naked

John, nicknamed "the disciple whom Jesus loved," records a stunning scene on the shores of the Sea of Tiberias (John 21). Here, after the resurrection of Jesus, a restless Peter tells the other disciples that he's going fishing; six of them join him, fishing all night and catching nothing. At daybreak they see a man on the shore, calling to them: "Children, you do not have any fish, do you?" Nope. So the man tells them to cast their net on the right side of the boat—"and then they were not able to haul it in because of the great number of fish." As they are fighting to bring the catch into the boat John points to the shore and says: "It is the Lord!" And Peter scrunches up his eyes to confirm that it's Jesus, and then explodes with desire...

He's stripped naked for work, because that's how fisherman did it back in the day. But he must get to Jesus NOW. So he quickly ties his garment around his waist and, like a child rushing to meet his soldier daddy who's home from the war, plunges into the choppy waters and swims furiously to shore. The boat follows behind as Peter thrashes his way to Jesus, who is calmly building a fire so they can have breakfast together. When Peter arrives, panting and naked and dripping wet, he stands before Jesus. In the garden, before the fall, Adam and Eve stood before God "naked and unashamed." Now Peter stands again before God, naked and unashamed. Maybe he's the first person since the great fall to do it.

The self-consciousness that sin and betrayal creates in us is obliterated when our passion for Jesus overshadows our fear of embarrassment.

RE-FRAME-ABLE

WHAT ARE YOU MOST ASHAMED OF? WHY DON'T
YOU WANT ANYONE TO DISCOVER YOUR SECRET
SHAME? MAYBE BECAUSE IT'S A SECRET AND
IT'S SHAMEFUL! AND... YOU PROBABLY FEAR
THEIR REACTION TO YOUR SECRET. SO IT'S
BETTER JUST TO KEEP IT A SECRET.

BUT WHAT IF IT'S NOT BETTER TO KEEP
SECRET STUFF, SECRET? WHAT IF KEEPING IT
SECRET ONLY MAKES IT MORE DAMAGING?
WHAT IF THERE'S SOMEBODY WHO WE CAN BE
COMPLETELY HONEST WITH? WHAT IF THERE
WAS SOMEBODY WITH WHOM WE COULD BE
"STRIPPED NAKED"... TOTALLY HONEST AND
UNASHAMED? YOU KNOW WHERE WE'RE GOING
WITH THIS. HIS NAME IS JESUS.

HE WAITS ON THE SHORE FOR YOU. GO
AHEAD, SHARE WITH HIM NOW.

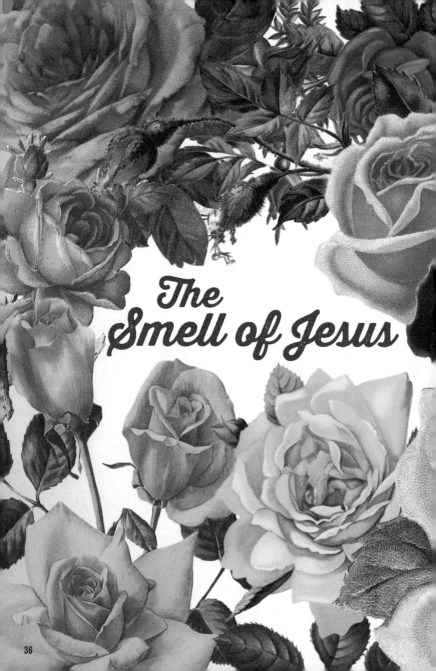

The
Smell of Jesus

Jesus *does* have a smell... It's a smell that would remind *you* of fresh-baked bread, but to others it smells more like a freshly deposited steaming pile of... poo. "For we are a fragrance of Christ to God among those who are being saved and among those who are perishing: to the one an aroma from death to death, to the other an aroma from life to life" (2 Corinthians 2:15-16). The fragrance of Christ—"life to life"—is a scent we want to wallow in. And the closer we get to him the more his smell rubs off on us.

We don't want mere data about Jesus—we want to experience him often enough and truly enough that his smell rubs off on us. Think about Jesus' encounter with the "woman at the well" in John 4. After she mistakes what he's offering her (she thinks he intends to draw water from the well for her), Jesus tells her the water from Jacob's Well is nothing compared to the "living water" of himself. He wants her to drink of him—an invitation to know him so intimately that her thirst (longing for something more in life) would be quenched forever. He wants his smell to rub off on her. When I (Rick) was dating my wife I used one of her old T-shirts as a pillowcase, just because I loved her smell and wanted to be reminded of it. And that's why we read the Bible—to remind ourselves of the smell of Jesus.

RE-FRAME-ABLE

RICK, THIS IS KURT... UMM, DID YOUR FUTURE WIFE KNOW YOU WERE USING ONE OF HER SHIRTS AS A PILLOWCASE? BECAUSE THAT'S JUST WEIRD!

OR IS IT?

WHEN YOU TRULY LOVE SOMEBODY YOU WANT TO BE CLOSE-YOU'LL EVEN FIND SOME PRETTY CREATIVE WAYS TO ACCOMPLISH THAT GOAL! WE'RE GUESSING THAT MOST OF YOU ARE READING THIS BOOK BECAUSE YOU LOVE JESUS AND WANT TO GET A LITTLE CLOSER TO HIM. YOU'VE PROBABLY NEVER PUT IT IN THESE WORDS, BUT THE REALITY IS THAT YOU WANT TO GET CLOSE ENOUGH TO JESUS TO SMELL HIM-AND AS YOU DO, YOU HOPE TO SMELL A LITTLE MORE LIKE HIM, TOO. YOU MAY BE THINKING, "OK, GUYS...THAT'S JUST WEIRD!"

OR IS IT?

No More Funhouse Mirrors

We're surrounded by mirrors—unless you're a supermodel, I mean that symbolically... You have "mirrors" surrounding you that are trying to tell you who you are. And almost all of those mirrors give a false reflection of your true beauty—they include the number of Facebook friends you have, how fast a friend texts you back, how well you're attract the attention of the opposite sex, your mile-run time, your GPA, the prestige of your college acceptance letters, and on and on. And all of the mirrors that promise to define you, except for one, are funhouse mirrors. I mean, they're warped, and therefore reflect a false image of who you really are.

The one exception is Jesus. He alone is an accurate mirror for who you really are.

Jesus made his mission clear: "I have come to set captives free" (Luke 4:18). And what is our captivity? The false identity that our false mirrors form in us. This is evident when Jesus infuriates the Pharisees by offering forgiveness, not healing, to a paralytic man whose friends have brought him to the Master for a miraculous physical restoration. Jesus responds with this: "Which is easier: to say, 'Your sins are forgiven,' or to say, 'Get up and walk'"? (Matthew 9:5). Our core need is forgiveness that leads to a restored relationship with Jesus, who then reminds us of our true identity as God's beloved. We're as equally paralyzed by the damage to our identity as we are damaged by physical paralysis. Jesus wants to answer our deepest question: "Who am I, and am I treasured?"

RE-FRAME-ABLE

GO STAND IN FRONT OF A MIRROR...

NOW, DO YOU LIKE WHAT YOU SEE?

HOW HAVE THE VARIOUS "FUNHOUSE" MIRRORS IN YOUR LIFE TRIED TO MAKE YOU SEE IN YOURSELF?

HAVE THEY GIVEN YOU AN HONEST PICTURE OF WHO YOU REALLY ARE?

NOW PRETEND JESUS IS STANDING RIGHT NEXT TO YOU (ACTUALLY, YOU DON'T HAVE TO PRETEND; BECAUSE HE IS). HE SEES THE EXACT SAME PERSON IN THE MIRROR THAT YOU'RE STARING AT! BUT IS IT POSSIBLE HE SEES SOMETHING... SOMEBODY... DIFFERENT? IS IT POSSIBLE HE SEES THE TRUE YOU—THE "YOU" WHO IS LOVED, FORGIVEN, BLESSED, AND BEAUTIFUL? THE "YOU" WHO DOESN'T NEED TO WORK TO GAIN HIS APPROVAL?

WE'RE NOT SURE HOW YOUR DAY HAS BEEN SO FAR, OR WHAT'S IN STORE, BUT THIS LITTLE EXERCISE SHOULD HELP YOU FEEL READY TO TACKLE WHATEVER IS IN STORE!

The
Too-Familiar
Jesus

In his excellent book *Jesus Mean and Wild,* author Mark Galli describes what happened when a group of Laotian refugees asked if they could become members of the church he was pastoring. Because these Laotians had little knowledge of Jesus or the Bible, Galli offered to lead them through a study of Mark's Gospel. When Galli got to the passage where Jesus calms the storm, he asked the refugees to talk about the "storms" in their lives—their problems, worries, and struggles. The people looked confused and puzzled. Finally, one of the Laotian men asked, "Do you mean that Jesus actually calmed the wind and sea in the middle of a storm?"

Galli thought the man was struggling to accept such an over-the-top story, so he said: "Yes, but we should not get hung up on the details of the miracle. We should remember that Jesus can calm the storms in our lives." After another uncomfortable silence, another man spoke up: "Well, if Jesus calmed the wind and the waves, he must be a very powerful man!" The Laotians buzzed with excitement and worship. And while these newbie Christian refugees got all worked up about Jesus, Galli realized he'd so taken Jesus for granted that he'd missed him altogether.

When we think we know everything there is to know about Jesus, then we lose our wonder for his amazing-ness.

RE-FRAME-ABLE

REMEMBER TO TAKE THIS BOOK WITH YOU THE NEXT TIME YOU GO TO CHURCH OR YOUTH GROUP. WE DON'T WANT YOU TO TAKE JESUS FOR GRANTED, AND CHURCH IS A PLACE WHERE THAT SEEMS TO HAPPEN ALL TOO OFTEN. TRY THIS...WHILE YOU'RE DOING ALL THE "STUFF" THAT HAPPENS IN CHURCH (SINGING, LISTENING TO ANNOUNCEMENTS, TAKING OFFERING, PLAYING A GAME, LISTENING TO A LESSON) WRITE DOWN SOMETHING AWESOME ABOUT JESUS THAT THESE THINGS REMIND YOU OF-THINGS ABOUT JESUS THAT YOU'VE BECOME SO USED TO THAT YOU TAKE THEM FOR GRANTED...

The Thicker Life

We're living in an age best characterized by one word: "distraction." The world's most prevalent "disease" is boredom, and we've been working to eradicate it since the first cave-boy threw a rock at his sister. We're getting pretty close to getting rid of boredom, by the way. Our cell phones are like a "miracle drug" for it—they're an unending source of boredom-beating distractions. And in addition to our tech-toys and our social-media crushes, we're distracted by the blizzard of "shoulds" we hear every day and an impossible-to-handle torrent of information. Life is hyper-stimulating, and it's making us thin-of-soul.

In *Death by Suburb,* author Dave Goetz advocates something he calls "the thicker life." This way of living is marked by a primary pursuit of Jesus, an everyday dependence on his guidance, and a focus on serving the needs of others. "Thick" is a slow-down-and-pay-attention way of life, and it's in stark contrast to the speed-up-and-distract way of life that's our "new norm." To live a "thicker" life, we start by adopting a "beeline" mentality whenever we read the Bible. No matter what part of the Bible we're reading, we're always wondering how it points to Jesus or prepares us for Jesus or helps us understand Jesus better. The effect of finding the beeline to Jesus every time we crack open the Bible (or tap on our Bible app) is that we learn to follow every road until we end up in "the metropolis of Christ." We slow down long enough to clear our distractions and pay attention to Jesus, no matter where we're reading in the Bible.

WHEN'S THE LAST TIME YOU "UN-PLUGGED" ON PURPOSE? THE LAST TIME YOU WENT A FULL DAY WITHOUT CHECKING YOUR PHONE FOR TEXTS OR UPLOADING A PICTURE OR PLAYING WITH YOUR FAVORITE APP?

TIME FOR A REFRAMING ONE-DAY EXPERIMENT.

FOR ONE DAY, LEAVE YOUR PHONE AT HOME. TRY MAKING YOURSELF MUCH MORE PRESENT AND AWARE OF THE PEOPLE AROUND YOU THAN YOU NORMALLY DO.

- WHAT'S SOMETHING YOU'VE NEVER NOTICED BEFORE ABOUT A FRIEND?

- LOOK FOR A "JESUS MOMENT" OPPORTUNITY HE PRESENTS FOR YOU TO SERVE.

- WHAT'S SOMETHING ABOUT JESUS YOU NEVER NOTICED BEFORE?

NOTHING WRONG WITH YOUR CELL PHONE-IT'S JUST GOOD TO TAKE A REFRAMING BREAK EVERY NOW AND THEN!

If You Don't Need Him,

A few summers ago, Colorado youth pastor Josh Jones launched his youth group out of its summer-mission-trip rut. Every year he and his students would load up the church's 12-passenger van and head south for the 28-hour trek to Mexico and a weeklong work camp. And every year, as they traveled through countless towns on the way to their mission location, they saw dozens of opportunities to serve people that they were forced to pass by. Those "on the way" possibilities planted the seed of an idea in Josh. His group had already spent

RE-FRAME-ABLE

WE READ STORIES LIKE THE ONE ABOVE AND IT SOUNDS CRAZY—THIS IDEA OF TOTAL DEPENDENCE ON JESUS. BUT BACK IN THE DAY (IN THE EARLY DAYS OF CHRISTIANITY) THAT WAY OF LIVING WAS PRETTY NORMAL. THE EARLY FOLLOWERS OF JESUS HAD NO IDEA WHAT THEY WERE GETTING INTO OR WHERE IT WOULD LEAD.

BUT TODAY, WITH WELL-ORGANIZED CHURCHES AND YOUTH GROUPS HELPING US NAVIGATE OUR FAITH, SOMETIMES IT SEEMS LIKE WE DON'T EVEN NEED TO TRUST JESUS. BUT WHAT IF THERE WASN'T CHURCH? WHAT IF YOU DIDN'T HAVE A YOUTH GROUP FOR SUPPORT?

You Won't Know Him

months studying all the ways that followers of Jesus depend upon the guidance of the Holy Spirit (aka "the Spirit of Jesus") in their everyday life. Why not plan something called The Magical Mystery tour—a mission trip that has no planned destination?

Here's how it worked, according to Josh: "Because we'd been learning about dependence on the Holy Spirit, we decided we didn't need a 'destination' for our trip. Simply, we decided to ask the Holy Spirit to lead us to where he wanted us

to go... We had no destination in mind and no plans for where we were going to stay or eat—all we had were a lot of 'what if's' and a trailer-full of supplies hitched to our van." In the end, Josh's group spent a week on the road trying to "listen better" to the Spirit of Jesus, then respond by *doing something*. They helped dozens of people along the way who had real needs—needs the Spirit knew about. And the big side benefit is that they got to know Jesus much, much better, simply because they were depending on him so much. And that's the thing about getting to know Jesus: If you don't need him, you won't know him.

- HOW WOULD YOU APPROACH LIFE DIFFERENTLY IF IT WAS JUST YOU AND JESUS?

- HAS BEING PART OF A YOUTH GROUP ACTUALLY CAUSED YOU TO RELY ON CHRIST LESS? HOW?

- TODAY, PRAY... "JESUS, TODAY I'M GONNA LET YOU LEAD ME—TOTALLY, COMPLETELY. I'M NOT DOING ANYTHING THAT I DON'T FEEL YOU LEADING ME TO DO."

Scaring Yourself for Good

After I (Rick) graduated from college, I joined an international training school to learn how to connect with people and talk to them about Jesus. One night in Sicily, during an outreach event, a woman came screaming and flailing into our midst, apparently possessed by a demon. I'm not kidding—it was like something out of a movie. There was no time to consult with demon-dealing experts at that point. My friends and I had to trust that the Spirit of Jesus would show us what to do right then. So we prayed and asked for help. Then we prayed over this scary woman as best we could, trusting Jesus to assert his authority over any oppressive spirits. And the woman promptly stopped screaming and frothing and thrashing. She became calm, as if someone had flipped a switch inside her. We stood amazed at the power of God, and we were drawn more deeply into relationship with Jesus because we'd sort-of partnered to pull this whole thing off.

In practical terms, depending on Jesus means scaring ourselves, in a good way. It means taking risks to serve others when the Spirit of Jesus nudges us. It might mean volunteering to lead something that you'd normally not lead, or serving in a setting that's far outside your comfort zone, or reaching out to people whose problems are beyond your ability to solve, or talking to your friends about the real Jesus.

RE-FRAME-ABLE

DID YOU KNOW THAT RESEARCHERS HAVE FOUND THAT THREE-QUARTERS (75%) OF ALL ADULT CHRISTIANS HAVE NEVER TOLD ANYBODY ELSE ABOUT JESUS? AND FEAR WAS THEIR #1 EXCUSE.

FEAR OF REJECTION, FEAR OF BEING TEASED, FEAR OF NOT HAVING ALL THE ANSWERS TO QUESTIONS THAT COME UP.

IT'S HUMAN NATURE TO TRY TO AVOID STUFF THAT SCARES US. BUT WHAT IF FULLY FOLLOWING JESUS MEANS BEING WILLING TO PUT OURSELVES IN SCARY SITUATIONS FOR THE GOOD OF OTHERS?

IS THERE SOMETHING YOU'VE FELT NUDGED TO DO IN THE PAST FOR CHRIST, BUT WERE SCARED TO DO?

WRITE DOWN SOMETHING THAT SCARES YOU THAT'S CONNECTED TO YOUR RELATIONSHIP WITH JESUS:

WHAT'S ONE WAY YOU COULD TAKE A BITE OUT OF YOUR FEAR TODAY—EVEN IF IT'S JUST A NIBBLE? WRITE YOUR IDEA HERE:

My (Rick here) friend Ron Belsterling, who teaches about youth ministry at Nyack College in New York and serves as a volunteer youth leader, decided to replace his youth group's traditional overseas mission trip with a local inner-city outreach. One night the group looked out their hotel window and saw two men viciously kicking a woman who was high on drugs, and therefore unable to defend herself or run away. Ron turned to his suburban, middle-class teenagers and asked, "What are we going to do about this?" His students said, "Well, we can't go down there!" And Ron answered, "Why not? *Down there* is where Jesus would be."

The students responded: "What can we do? The only thing we know how to do is sing!" (Most of the students on the outreach were part of the church's respected youth choir.) Ron fired back, "Well, let's go down there and sing, then. We'll give what Jesus has given us to give." So the whole group trooped down to the street and started singing. The two guys kicking the woman looked up, startled, and ran away in fear. The woman crawled across the street and lay down in the middle of the kids as they sang. That night, those students followed the beeline to Jesus that Ron found for them. They learned what it's like to follow the nudge of the Spirit and offer rescue to a woman in trouble, just as Jesus did with the woman caught in adultery in John 8.

Where Would Jesus Be?

RE-FRAME-ABLE

TAKE A MINUTE AND READ THE JESUS ENCOUNTER IN JOHN 8 THAT RICK JUST MENTIONED. TALK ABOUT JESUS BEING "REFRAMED"! YOU SEE, BACK IN THE DAY, A WOMAN WHO WAS CAUGHT IN A SEXUAL RELATIONSHIP WITH A MAN SHE WASN'T MARRIED TO COULD BE PUT TO DEATH—IT WAS THE LAW (CREATED AND ENFORCED BY THE RELIGIOUS LEADERS). JESUS, AS A SIGNIFICANT RELIGIOUS LEADER, WOULD'VE BEEN TOTALLY WITHIN THE LAW TO NOT ONLY LOOK THE OTHER WAY, BUT TO PICK UP A ROCK OF HIS OWN!

BUT JESUS REFRAMED THE RULES OF THE GAME (WHICH HE HAD A FANTASTIC HABIT OF DOING). HE ALLOWED GRACE, LOVE, FORGIVENESS, AND A SECOND CHANCE TO BE MORE IMPORTANT THAN JUDGMENT AND PUNISHMENT.

SADLY, 2,000 YEARS LATER, MANY CHRISTIANS ARE KNOWN MORE FOR THE STONES THEY LIKE TO THROW AT OTHER PEOPLE THAN FOR THE GRACE THEY SHOW. IF YOU ARE A FOLLOWER OF JESUS, IT'S TIME TO PUT DOWN THE ROCKS!

· THINK ABOUT ONE "ROCK" YOU'VE BEEN HOLDING ON TO IN YOUR LIFE—WHAT WOULD IT LOOK LIKE FOR YOU TO RELEASE THAT ROCK AND LET IT DROP TO THE GROUND?

· WHAT WOULD YOU HAVE TO SAY OR DO TO "DROP IT"?

Anything

Can Happen

NEXT

We can learn a lot about Jesus if we pay better attention to how he interacted with people. For example, in Matthew 10 Jesus sent out his 12 best friends on their first ministry trip without him. They went out in pairs, and Jesus made sure they'd feel very, very dependent on his grace and provision as they traveled: "Do not get any gold or silver or copper to take with you in your belts—no bag for the journey or extra shirt or sandals or a staff, for the worker is worth his keep" (Matthew 10:9-10, NIV).

When his disciples returned to download what happened on their ministry adventures, they told Jesus they were astonished by how God's Spirit had moved through them: "Lord, even the demons submit to us in your name." And Jesus reminded his disciples that the power they experienced when they depended on his Spirit came directly from him (so don't get too impressed with yourselves). If you believe anything can happen because of your deepening dependence on Jesus, then it's quite likely that *anything will happen!*

RE-FRAME-ABLE

WRITE DOWN 10 THINGS THAT ARE MOST IMPORTANT TO YOU.

1.
2.
3.
4.
5.
6.
7.
8.
9.
10.

NOW, PICK TWO OR THREE AND, NEXT TO THEM, WRITE THE ANSWERS TO THESE QUESTIONS:

"HOW WOULD YOUR LIFE BE DIFFERENT IF YOU HAD TO LEAVE THIS BEHIND?"

"IN WHAT WAYS WOULD LIFE WITHOUT THIS THING MAKE YOU MORE DEPENDENT ON JESUS?"

"IF JESUS GAVE YOU THE SAME INSTRUCTIONS HE GAVE HIS DISCIPLES-TO BASICALLY LEAVE EVERYTHING BEHIND-WOULD YOU BE ABLE TO LEAVE THIS ONE?"

A LOT OF PEOPLE THINK THAT FOLLOWING JESUS MEANS THAT HE'S SOMEHOW OBLIGATED TO GIVE THEM EVERYTHING THEY WANT-THAT THEY'LL NEVER HAVE TO SACRIFICE OR GO WITHOUT. THEY SEE JESUS AS SOME SORT OF HEAVENLY VENDING MACHINE DISPENSING WHAT THEY WANT, WHEN THEY WANT IT. BUT JESUS REFRAMES THAT THINKING! SOMETIMES GOING WITH CHRIST MEANS GOING WITHOUT OTHER STUFF! BUT GOING WITHOUT MEANS WE CREATE SPACE FOR JESUS TO PUT SOMETHING IN OUR LIFE WE NEVER KNEW WE WANTED...

The Not-So-Nice Jesus

Most people describe Jesus in ways that have little relationship to what he really said and did. They think he's a nice, good man—kind of a Barney for grown-ups. And that isn't the Jesus of the Bible.

Yes, Jesus was a "nice guy" when he healed people or fed them miraculously or saved them from certain death or demon possession. He was certainly kind to children and went out of his way to be gentle with the brokenhearted. But he was also so fierce with hypocritical religious leaders and used such profane lan-

RE-FRAME-ABLE

"JESUS IS MORE EVERYTHING THAN THE WAY HE'S TYPICALLY DESCRIBED."

THAT MEANS JESUS IS:

- MORE OF A REVOLUTIONARY THAN WE PROBABLY THINK.
- MORE OF A TROUBLEMAKER THAN WE PROBABLY THINK.
- MORE LOVING THAN WE PROBABLY THINK.
- MORE PASSIONATE ABOUT HIS CAUSE THAN WE PROBABLY THINK.
- MORE OF A RADICAL THAN WE PROBABLY THINK.
- MORE OF A GOOD SHEPHERD THAN WE PROBABLY THINK.
- MORE OF A... WELL, MORE EVERYTHING THAN YOU PROBABLY THINK!

IF JESUS WAS MORE OF A TROUBLEMAKER (THE GOOD KIND!) THAN YOU PROBABLY THINK, WHAT CAN YOU LEARN FROM HIM AS YOU FOLLOW HIS WAYS?

IF JESUS IS MORE PASSIONATE ABOUT HIS CAUSE THAN YOU PROBABLY THINK, WHAT CAN YOU LEARN FROM HIM AS YOU PURSUE YOUR PASSIONS?

IF JESUS IS MORE LOVING THAN YOU PROBABLY THINK, WHAT CAN YOU LEARN FROM HIM ABOUT LOVING THOSE AROUND YOU?

guage to describe them that they conspired to execute him. And Jesus wasn't a "nice guy" when he labeled a Canaanite woman who sought healing for her daughter a "dog," or (of course) when he used a whip to clear the Temple of the conniving money-changers, or when he responded to Peter's pledge to protect him from harm by calling him "Satan."

The Jesus of the Bible is more dangerous than nice; actually, he's more everything than the way he's typically described.

The great author, journalist, and thinker G.K. Chesterton once said: "If you meet the Jesus of the Gospels, you must redefine what love is, or you won't be able to stand him." This is true, because Jesus was a difficult person—a lot of people were uncomfortable in his presence and scandalized by things he said and did. It's hard to "stand" Jesus if you're really paying attention to what he did and said. He is the most disruptive person who ever walked the earth. And he is so much better than our typical descriptions of him—so much more than a dispenser of life lessons or a teller of cute fables. He's the greatest lover the world has ever known...

There are plenty of nice people doing nice things in the world, but we wouldn't give our lives to follow them. The leaders at Vintage Church in North Carolina decided to satirize the "fake Jesus" most of us have come to know—to chip away at our wrong notions of Jesus so we can be reintroduced to him. They took a ridiculous old film about Jesus, extracted four scenes from it, then recorded their own dialogue to replace the original audio. The result is hilarious (check out the videos on YouTube by searching for "Vintage Church Jesus Videos"). They gave Jesus a falsetto Mr. Rogers voice, making him the wimpy Jesus so many of us imagine anyway. And they portrayed him as a distant rule-keeper who's out of touch with real life. Humor is like a mirror—it reflects back to us some of the silly things we've come to believe, showing us how silly they really are.

RE-FRAME-ABLE

BY NOW YOU ARE PROBABLY BEGINNING TO UNDERSTAND WHAT WE ARE TRYING TO DO IN THIS LITTLE BOOK: WE WANT YOU TO LOOK AT JESUS DIFFERENTLY. TO "REFRAME" HIM!

BUT THAT'S NOT EASY.

IT'S NOT EASY BECAUSE YOU'VE PROBABLY SPENT 10-15 YEARS IN SUNDAY SCHOOL CLASSES AND YOUTH GROUP BIBLE STUDIES LEARNING ABOUT THE GENTLE, LOVING, "TURN THE OTHER CHEEK" JESUS—THINKING OF HIM AS A RADICAL REVOLUTIONARY WHO YELLED AT RELIGIOUS LEADERS AND GOT FRUSTRATED WITH HIS OWN DISCIPLES ISN'T EASY. IT ISN'T EASY, BUT IT'S IMPORTANT BECAUSE YOU NEED TO KNOW WHAT YOU SIGNED UP FOR WHEN YOU DECIDED TO FOLLOW JESUS!

BEING A CHRISTIAN DOESN'T JUST MEAN BEING A FOLLOWER OF CHRIST; IT ALSO MEANS "STANDING HIM" AND STANDING WITH HIM. IT WON'T ALWAYS BE EASY, AND IT MAY NOT WIN YOU VERY MANY POPULARITY CONTESTS, BUT THE WORLD—YOUR FRIENDS AND YOUR ENEMIES— NEED TO SEE THE REAL DEAL. THEY NEED TO SEE THE REAL JESUS REFLECTED IN YOU.

WHEN PEOPLE "SEE JESUS IN YOU," WHAT PERSONALITY TRAITS OF JESUS DO THEY SEE?

Standing In

How do we get to the bottom of Jesus (so to speak)? Our goal is to move away from our lazy-thinking habits—"We kinda/sorta already know who Jesus is"—to pay attention more honestly to him. So we ask ourselves questions like these:

- What did Jesus really say/do here?

- When did he say/do it?

- Where did this all happen?

- Why did he say/do this?

- How did he say/do this?

As we question, we're digging for the truth about Jesus. We don't accept shallow explanations, and we don't move past the confusing or difficult things about Jesus too quickly. So often we treat the hard or confusing aspects of Jesus like mud puddles—we just jump over them. The key to understanding Jesus, though, is to stand in those mud puddles. We stay there and consider Jesus more deeply. To do that we follow G.K. Chesterton's advice—we redefine what love is because Jesus never did anything outside of love. We say to ourselves, "What Jesus said and did here is a perfect expression of love," then work backward from that assumption to understand how love was at work in him. We're determined to look Jesus full in the face—to not shy away from the things he did that make us uncomfortable, confused, or even angry. To stand in mud puddles until we know him better...

Mud Puddles

RE-FRAME-ABLE

GRAB YOUR BIBLE! IT'S TIME TO PRACTICE THE WHAT, WHEN, WHERE, WHY, HOW EXERCISE. LOOK UP THE FOLLOWING THINGS JESUS SAID AND ASK THE FIVE QUESTIONS OUTLINED IN THE PARAGRAPH TO THE LEFT YOU JUST READ. ANSWERS MAY NOT COME EASILY, AND THEY MAY NOT EVEN BE TOTALLY RIGHT, BUT THAT'S OK–YOU ARE PRACTICING THE PRACTICE OF GETTING TO KNOW JESUS IN NEW WAYS!

TWO TIPS TO HELP YOU OUT:

- DON'T JUST READ THE PORTION OF SCRIPTURE WE PROVIDE FOR YOU–READ "AROUND" IT. IN OTHER WORDS, READ IT IN CONTEXT. THAT MEANS READING A FEW VERSES BEFORE AND AFTER TO GET A BETTER SENSE OF WHAT WAS HAPPENING WHEN JESUS SAID WHAT HE SAID.

- DON'T VIEW THIS AS AN EXERCISE OR AN "ASSIGNMENT" (IT'S NOT GEOMETRY!). INSTEAD, LOOK AT THIS AS AN OPPORTUNITY TO GET TO KNOW THE ONE YOU LOVE IN NEW, MORE INTIMATE WAYS.

HERE YOU GO!
MATTHEW 5:43-44
MATTHEW 16:24-25
MATTHEW 18:2-4

RE-FRAME-ABLE

OK, LET'S COMBINE WHAT WE DID ON THE LAST PAGE WITH "THE OPRAH QUESTION."

TURN BACK A PAGE AND LOOK AT THE PASSAGES AGAIN—REACQUAINT YOURSELF WITH WHAT YOU WROTE DOWN ABOUT EACH ONE. THEN, BASED ON YOUR ANSWERS, ASK YOURSELF:

· WHAT'S ONE THING I KNOW FOR SURE ABOUT JESUS FROM...

MATTHEW 5:43-44, MATTHEW 16:24-25, MATTHEW 18:2-4

When I (Rick) was a kid, every Bible printed the words of Jesus in red. It's a little less common today, but still popular. Red means "pay attention." That's why stop signs are always painted red. Designer Dustin W. Stout observes: "Red is the most eye-catching and exciting color in the entire spectrum. It's... exciting and demands attention. But did you know that the color red actually increases your heart rate? It is perfect for accent colors, calls to action, or anywhere you want to draw people's attention."

Bible publishers that print Jesus' words in red are intentionally focusing us on Jesus' words. Of course, all of the Bible is important to study, but the words of Jesus invite special attention because the Bible's whole narrative points to him. The "red stuff" in the Bible tells us to give greater focus to the things Jesus actually said. And my favorite way to do that is to "ask the Oprah Question." Near the back of every O Magazine, Oprah asks her celebrity guests this brilliant question: "What's one thing you know for sure?" Let's morph this question a little to this: "Based on this Scripture passage, what's one thing you know for sure about Jesus?" Every time you read something Jesus said or did, ask the Oprah question—this is a simple way to know him more intimately.

HERE'S SOMETHING ELSE WE KNOW FOR SURE: THAT JESUS WANTS US TO BE PEOPLE WHO PUT SCRIPTURE INTO ACTION IN OUR LIVES, NOT JUST PEOPLE WHO KNOW WHAT IT SAYS (JAMES 1:22-25). SO THE MOST IMPORTANT QUESTION TO ASK YOURSELF IS THIS:

"NOW THAT I KNOW THIS FOR SURE ABOUT JESUS, WHAT DOES HE WANT ME TO DO ABOUT IT?"

Jesus Did
← ≪ ≫ →
Jesus Didn't

Another way to focus on the red stuff (or to pay peculiar attention to the things Jesus said and did) is a simple habit we call the "Jesus Did/Jesus Didn't" practice. Here's a taste of how this works. Get a piece of paper and something to write with, then choose five or six "red" verses from one of the four Gospels—Matthew, Mark, Luke, or John. On your paper, draw a line down the middle to create two columns. Label the first column "Jesus Did" and the other "Jesus Didn't." See below.

Then read through those verses, looking for things Jesus embraced, advised, or did, and list them under the "Jesus Did" column. Then, to spark your thinking even more, go back through that list and brainstorm the opposite of each thing you've listed. For example, if you write, "He healed people of sickness" on the "Jesus Did" side, you can write, "He didn't ignore or leave sick those who came to him seeking healing." This is a sample of how this could look with the start of John 6:

Jesus Did

Jesus chooses when he wants to be with crowds and when he wants to retreat with his friends.

Jesus tests our faith so see how we react to challenges.

Jesus Didn't

Jesus doesn't let others determine what he needs.

Jesus doesn't always make it easy to follow him.

Once you've done this on paper a couple of times, your brain will start to think this way without using the paper. It'll grow into a normal way of thinking—"What did Jesus really do here?" and "What didn't Jesus do here?"

RE-FRAME-ABLE

NOW THAT WAS A GREAT LITTLE EXERCISE! IN FACT, IF YOU HAVEN'T DONE IT YET, DON'T KEEP READING THIS PART. SERIOUSLY, STOP NOW. SERIOUSLY.

THE CLASSIC QUESTION "WHAT WOULD JESUS DO?" IS WORTH ASKING—IT'S IMPORTANT TO TRY TO EXPLORE WHAT WE THINK JESUS MIGHT DO IN REAL-LIFE SITUATIONS. BUT IF YOU'RE LIKE MOST PEOPLE, YOU'VE NEVER ASKED THE OPPOSITE QUESTION: "WHAT WOULD JESUS NOT DO?" (WWJND) IN ANY GIVEN SITUATION. IT'S NOT AS CATCHY, AND WON'T SELL AS MANY COOL LITTLE RUBBER BRACELET THINGIES, BUT IT'S EQUALLY IMPORTANT. AND THAT'S WHY IT'S SO IMPORTANT FOR YOU TO GET TO KNOW THE REAL JESUS; BECAUSE THE REAL JESUS IS JUST AS POWERFUL, JUST AS WONDERFUL, JUST AS WORTHY OF OUR LOYALTY BECAUSE OF THE THINGS HE DIDN'T DO AS HE IS FOR THE STUFF HE ACTUALLY DID.

WHAT WOULD JESUS NOT DO? WHAT ARE YOU DOING—STUFF THAT MAYBE YOU ASSUME JESUS WOULD DO—THAT MAY NOT BE SO JESUS-LIKE AFTER ALL?

When we focus on the things we *know* Jesus did, rather than take wild guesses about what he'd do if he were in our present circumstances,

we anchor our relationship with him in reality. Check out this little sampler of how Jesus interacted with people who sought him out for healing—notice what Jesus says and does, and doesn't say or do:

Matthew 9:22 (NIV)—"Jesus turned and saw her. 'Take heart, daughter,' he said, 'your faith has healed you.' And the woman was healed from that

Matthew 15:28 (NIV)—"Then Jesus said to her, 'Woman, you have great faith! Your request is granted.' And her daughter was healed from that very hour."

John 5:13 (NIV)—"The man who was healed had no idea who it was, for Jesus had slipped away into the crowd that was there."

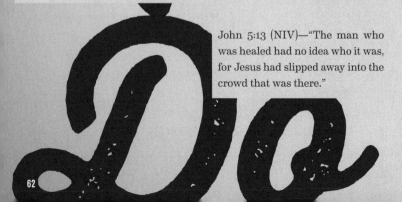

Do you notice how Jesus healed people—cared for their most desperate needs—without *requiring them* to follow him or thank him or even believe that he was the Messiah? When we love people simply because they need to be loved, with no strings attached, we're doing what Jesus did. And when we do the things Jesus did, depending on his Spirit for the strength and courage to do them, we understand his heart more deeply.

RE-FRAME-ABLE

LOVING OTHERS WITH NO STRINGS ATTACHED. THAT IS A TOUGH CONCEPT TO GRASP BECAUSE WE LIVE IN A WORLD WHERE JUST ABOUT EVERYTHING HAS STRINGS ATTACHED, AND LOTS OF THEM.

YOU GET AN INCREASE IN ALLOWANCE IF YOU DO YOUR CHORES, DON'T BREAK CURFEW, AND SO ON.

YOU MAKE THE TEAM IF YOU DO WELL IN TRYOUTS.

YOU GET THE JOB IF YOUR INTERVIEW GOES SMOOTHLY.

YOU GROW IN POPULARITY IF YOU ACT THE WAY THE CROWD EXPECTS.

THERE'S A CERTAIN AMOUNT OF GIVE-AND-TAKE IN LIFE THAT'S GOOD, NATURAL, AND HEALTHY. BUT SOMETIMES, AS FOLLOWERS OF JESUS, OUR CALLING IS TO SIMPLY GIVE WITHOUT TAKING IN RETURN. NOW, IT'S NOT AS IF JESUS NEVER EXPECTED ANYTHING IN RETURN… HE CERTAINLY WASN'T AFRAID TO ASK HIS FOLLOWERS FOR A CERTAIN LEVEL OF OBEDIENCE AND COMMITMENT. BUT FROM THOSE WHO WERE ON THE OUTSIDE, THOSE WHO WERE NEW TO JESUS' WAYS, HE EXPECTED ALMOST NOTHING. HE JUST GAVE, HE JUST HEALED, HE JUST LOVED. THAT'S WHAT HE DID.

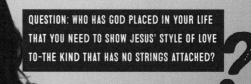

QUESTION: WHO HAS GOD PLACED IN YOUR LIFE THAT YOU NEED TO SHOW JESUS' STYLE OF LOVE TO-THE KIND THAT HAS NO STRINGS ATTACHED?

Obliterating the Distance

When you think about all the cultural stuff you and your friends are into—the music, movies, social media services, websites, TV shows, and books—how do you know what's "OK/not OK" for you to get into as a Jesus-believer? Well, here's one thing we know—Jesus never distanced himself from his culture. In fact, he so closely attached himself to "worldly" people and environments that some claimed he was "of the world" himself. If we think we're keeping ourselves "holy" by cutting ourselves off from the culture we live in, we're fooling ourselves. Jesus got close to culture, then praised what was good and exposed what was bad. He did not fear sin; he got close enough to it to slap it in the face.

Jesus refused to split himself in two—living one way when he was around religious people and totally different when he wasn't. He lived a "congruent" life—equally comfortable in the darkness and in the light. That's because his outside circumstances and influences did not define him—he maintained his core identity no matter who or what he was around. He responded to cultural influences by either celebrating them or subverting them, not running from them. So, he condemned the hypocritical cultural practices of the Pharisees in their presence, and he celebrated traditional cultural festivals with his presence. He didn't picket the homes of sinners; he invited himself to dinner with them.

RE-FRAME-ABLE ON THE CHART BELOW, MAKE A LIST OF SOME CULTURAL "STUFF" YOU ARE INTO, THEN TAKE A MINUTE TO DO SOMETHING WITH EACH THING THAT MOST TEENAGERS HAVE NEVER DONE:

EVALUATE IT.

WHAT'S AWESOME ABOUT IT, WHAT'S NOT-SO-AWESOME ABOUT IT, AND ONE WAY YOU CAN USE THAT THING TO BRING LIGHT INTO THE DARKNESS OF THE PEOPLE AROUND YOU. IN OTHER WORDS, HOW CAN YOU USE IT TO HELP NUDGE SOMEONE TOWARD JESUS?

MY STUFF	AWESOME	NOT SO AWESOME

Primary Pursuit

Jesus absolutely loved to ask questions—if you count every question he asked in the four Gospels (Matthew, Mark, Luke, and John) you come up with an astonishing number—287! And these weren't easy-answer questions—for example:

- "Which is easier: to say to the paralytic, 'Your sins are forgiven,' or to say, 'Get up, take your mat and walk?'" (Mark 2:9, NIV).

- "Salt is good, but if it loses its saltiness, how can you make it salty again?" (Mark 9:50, NIV).

- "Why do you call me good?" (Mark 10:18, NIV).

As we get to know Jesus more deeply, we learn that he loves to throw questions at us that entice us to pursue him, *because he loves to be pursued*. He drove home that truth for his disciples with this little parable: "Imagine what would happen if you went to a friend in the middle of the night and said, 'Friend, lend me three loaves of bread. An old friend traveling through just showed up, and I don't have a thing on hand.' The friend answers from his bed, 'Don't bother me. The door's locked; my children are all down for the night; I can't get up to give you anything.' But let me tell you, even if he won't get up because he's a friend, if you stand your ground, knocking and waking all the neighbors, he'll finally get up and get you whatever you need" (Luke 11:5-8, THE MESSAGE).

Persistence is the key—Jesus is inviting us to be persistent in "knocking on his door." And his "primary pursuit" question is this: "Who do you say that I am?"

—SUBMIT ANSWER HERE—

N° 277238

JAMES 1:22 SAYS: "BUT DON'T JUST LISTEN TO GOD'S WORD. YOU MUST DO WHAT IT SAYS. OTHERWISE, YOU ARE ONLY FOOLING YOURSELVES."

SCRIPTURE MAKES IT CLEAR OVER AND OVER AGAIN (THE VERSE ABOVE IS JUST ONE EXAMPLE) THAT SIMPLY LISTENING ISN'T ENOUGH–IF WE KNOW SOMETHING ABOUT GOD OR JESUS OR HIS TRUTHS BUT DON'T DO ANYTHING ABOUT IT... IT'S WORTHLESS.

SO MERELY ANSWERING JESUS' QUESTION "WHO DO YOU SAY I AM" ISN'T ENOUGH. IN FACT, LOTS OF CHRISTIANS CAN ANSWER THAT QUESTION ONE WAY OR ANOTHER:

"JESUS IS THE SON OF GOD"

"JESUS IS THE MESSIAH"

RE-FRAME-ABLE

"JESUS IS THE FORGIVER OF SINS"

"JESUS IS GOD IN THE FLESH"

AND WHILE THESE "TRUTHS" ARE GOOD TO KNOW, MERE KNOWING IS NOT GOOD ENOUGH! KNOWING JESUS MUST LEAD TO A NEW WAY OF THINKING, A NEW WAY OF REACTING, A NEW WAY OF RELATING... A NEW WAY OF LIVING!

IMPORTANT QUESTION: WHO DO YOU SAY JESUS IS?

MORE IMPORTANT QUESTION: HOW DOES YOUR KNOWLEDGE OF JESUS INFLUENCE THE WAY YOU LIVE YOUR LIFE?

Three Questions

Jesus is the best-known, least-known person in history. I mean, he's easily the most famous person who ever lived. And yet, even though so many of us think we know him, so few of us have slowed down long enough to consider what he actually said and did. That's pretty much the only way you can get to know someone for who they really are—notice what they say and what they do. And because we've already decided that we pretty much know who Jesus is, we've inoculated ourselves from actually knowing him. An inoculation gives you a little bit of the sickness you're trying to avoid so that your immune system will already be in attack mode. We know a little bit about Jesus, and that little bit "inoculates" us against the reality of who he is.

Here's a simple way to counteract that inoculation—whenever you're reading or discussing a Scripture passage that includes things Jesus said and did, ask yourself these three questions:

1 "What did Jesus really say?" (*Think of what was happening around him.*)

2 "What did Jesus really do?" (*What impact did his words or actions have on the people around him?*)

3 "How did people really experience Jesus?" (*Look for their emotional reactions.*)

Start asking these questions all the time, and soon you'll be pursuing Jesus with the sort of persistence that *unlocks* him.

RE-FRAME-ABLE

AS YOU BEGIN TO PURSUE JESUS
IN A WAY THAT UNLOCKS THE REAL
HIM, YOU WILL EVENTUALLY HAVE
OPPORTUNITIES TO SHOW THE REAL
JESUS TO YOUR FRIENDS. THIS IS
ACTUALLY AN AMAZING OPPORTUNITY
BECAUSE MOST OF YOUR FRIENDS HAVE
A VERY LIMITED (AND PROBABLY HIGHLY
INACCURATE) PICTURE OF CHRIST.

HERE'S WHAT WE WANT YOU
TO DO TODAY—THINK OF A FRIEND
WHO YOU KNOW DOESN'T HAVE AN
ACCURATE PICTURE OF JESUS.

- HOW MIGHT YOU SHOW HIM/
  HER JESUS' KIND OF LOVE?

- HOW MIGHT YOU SHOW HIM/HER
  JESUS' KIND OF FORGIVENESS?

- HOW MIGHT YOU SHOW HIM/HER
  JESUS' KIND OF COMMITMENT?

IN OTHER WORDS, AS YOU'RE
REFRAMING JESUS YOURSELF, HOW CAN
YOU HELP OTHERS REFRAME HIM, TOO?

The Jesus Push-Back

In our culture, "muscle fitness" is almost a religion. And that's a good thing...mostly. A focus on fitness in a culture of obesity—what could be wrong with that? Well, nothing, except there's a kind of fitness that's *even more important for our health*—the "muscle" most in need of strengthening is the one that fuels our critical thinking. I mean, our ability to "push back" against false things we hear or overhear about Jesus and the kingdom of God. Jesus himself did this all the time—you'll often find him saying something like: "You have heard it said that [fill in something that's passed off as the 'truth' in our culture], but I say [fill in a truth that Jesus has revealed about the kingdom of God]." He's showing his followers how to push back against lazy thinking and silly beliefs.

Pastor and author John Ortberg says: "In the Gospel of Mark, the scribes asked Jesus, 'Which commandment is the most important of all?' And Jesus quotes from Deuteronomy 6:5—'You shall love the Lord your God with all your heart and with all your soul and with all your might'—but added the admonition to love God 'with all your mind.' Why the addition? Cornelius Plantinga called this the Magna Carta for the Christian intellectual life. To love God with all our minds means we should think about him a lot—be interested in him."

Contrary to popular assumptions about followers of Christ, Jesus isn't an anti-intellectual. In fact, he's challenged us to maximize our minds in our pursuit of him, and in the way we live our lives for him.

RE-FRAME-ABLE

BACK IN THE DAY, THIS SLOGAN WAS POPULAR: "A MIND IS A TERRIBLE THING TO WASTE." AND IT'S AS TRUE TODAY AS IT WAS BACK THEN! GOD HAS GIVEN US AN INCREDIBLE BRAIN, AND WITH IT COMES THE ABILITY TO THINK OUTSIDE THE BOX-TO EXAMINE, QUESTION, WONDER, DOUBT, EVALUATE, AND A WHOLE BUNCH OF OTHER AWESOME STUFF.

IN ACTS 17:11 WE SEE AN EXAMPLE OF PEOPLE USING THEIR MINDS IN A GREAT WAY:

figure 1.1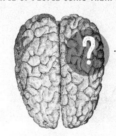

THEY PURPOSELY QUESTIONED WHETHER THE STUFF THEY WERE HEARING ABOUT JESUS WAS TRUE. AND GUESS WHAT? WE SHOULD DO THE SAME THING. JUST BECAUSE SOMEBODY SAYS SOMETHING ABOUT GOD, THE BIBLE, OR JESUS DOESN'T MAKE IT TRUE. AND JUST BECAUSE SOMEBODY SAYS IT IN A WAY THAT MAKES IT SOUND AUTHORITATIVE AND ACCURATE DOESN'T MAKE IT SO. WE NEED TO BE LIKE THE BEREANS IN ACTS AND QUESTION THE STUFF WE'RE HEARING, ASKING JESUS TO REVEAL THE TRUTH TO US ABOUT HIMSELF AND HIS WAYS.

YOU'VE PROBABLY ALREADY ASKED JESUS INTO YOUR HEART.

TODAY, ASK HIM INTO YOUR MIND AS WELL!

Lesser Gods

The documentary *The Armstrong Lie* explores the Lance Armstrong doping scandal from an unusual perspective—the legendary cyclist who denied using performance-enhancing drugs was later exposed as a cheater and stripped of his Tour de France victories. Instead of rehashing the facts of Armstrong's long deceit, the film explores why people for so long refused to accept the bitter truth about him. Armstrong was like a god to so many, and it's hard to give up on your god. The film is really about our relentless pursuit of "lesser gods"—we've always preferred "more approachable, more tangible" gods to Jesus.

In the aftermath of Nelson Mandela's funeral, for example, a young South African spoken-word artist named Thabiso Mohare wrote a poem in honor of the great anti-apartheid leader. Here's a portion of "An Ordinary Man":

RE-FRAME-ABLE

IN MATTHEW 6:33 JESUS BASICALLY SAYS THIS: "SEEK GOD AND HIS WAYS FIRST, AND HE'LL GIVE YOU EVERYTHING ELSE YOU NEED."

LATER, IN THE 19TH CHAPTER OF MATTHEW, JESUS TELLS A RICH YOUNG GUY THAT IN ORDER TO HAVE ETERNAL LIFE HE NEEDED TO SELL EVERYTHING, GIVE IT TO THE POOR, AND THEN FOLLOW HIM.

IN BOTH INSTANCES, JESUS WAS MAKING A VERY CLEAR POINT: HE WANTS, EXPECTS, AND DESERVES TO BE OUR GOD, AND WE AREN'T TO LET "LESSER GODS" TAKE HIS PLACE.

And we watched the world weep
For a giant bigger than myths
A life owned by many
Now free as the gods

"Worshipful" is the best way to describe the tone that infuses this poem. Makes sense, because Mandela was an amazing man. But it's easier and more acceptable to worship Nelson Mandela (or Mother Teresa or Steve Jobs or Justin Bieber or Oprah Winfrey) than it is to worship the "rock of offense" who is Jesus. He alone is worthy to be worshipped, but not because we're "supposed to." Everything Jesus said and did fits together into a perfect mirror of the God we can't see but long to know.

YOU KNOW WHERE THIS IS HEADING!

WHAT, OR WHO, HAVE YOU PLACED ABOVE JESUS IN YOUR LIFE? WHAT, OR WHO, WOULD BE HARD TO LET GO OF IF HE ASKED YOU TO? WHAT'S ONE SIMPLE THING YOU COULD DO TODAY TO REPRIORITIZE THINGS IN YOUR LIFE—TO ENSURE YOU'RE GIVING JESUS THE PRIORITY HE DESERVES?

Playing Sherlock

RE-FRAME-ABLE

OK, SHERLOCK, IT'S TIME FOR YOU TO PRACTICE WHAT WE'RE PREACHING! PICK ONE OF THE JESUS SCENARIOS WE LISTED ON THE RIGHT AND START INVESTIGATING. READ THE ENTIRE CHAPTER SO YOU GET SOME CONTEXT-RESEARCH IT ONLINE AND SEE WHAT BIBLE SCHOLARS AND OTHER SMART PEOPLE HAVE TO SAY ABOUT IT. THINK THROUGH SOME OF WHAT YOU KNOW TO BE TRUE ABOUT JESUS, THEN ASK YOURSELF: "HOW DOES WHAT I KNOW ABOUT JESUS HELP ME FIGURE OUT WHAT HE MEANT OR WHY HE DID WHAT HE JUST DID?"

YOU MAY NOT ALWAYS COME TO AN EASY ANSWER, AND SOME OF THE MYSTERIES OF JESUS' WAYS OF DOING THINGS MAY NEVER BE SOLVED-BUT THAT'S OK! THE POINT OF PLAYING SHERLOCK ISN'T ONLY ABOUT GETTING TO THE ANSWER, IT'S ABOUT LEARNING TO PAY CLOSER ATTENTION TO THINGS THAN WE USUALLY DO. IT'S LEARNING TO REFRAME JESUS!

RE-FRAME-ABLE

Another simple way to dig deeper into the heart of Jesus is to make believe you're like Sherlock Holmes—a master detective who's unraveling clues to a mystery. In this case, the "mystery" is Jesus. Here's how it works: Whenever you run across something Jesus says or does that doesn't make immediate sense, or something that makes you scratch your head, you study the problem to come up with possible solutions. For example:

- Why did Jesus treat the beggar woman in Matthew 15 so harshly?

- Why did Jesus tell his brothers he wouldn't attend a feast in Judea, then later go anyway? (John 7)

- Why did Jesus choose to heal the man born blind by spitting in the dirt, making a mud pack, then smearing it on the man's face and forcing him to walk through town to wash in a pool? (John 9)

- Why did Jesus choose Judas as a disciple? (Matthew 10)

- Why did Jesus tell Peter in advance that he would deny him? (Matthew 26)

We could go on and on. You already have what we might call a world-class "garbage meter"—an inner sense of what's true and what's not. But when you think of yourself as Sherlock Holmes whenever you read or hear something about Jesus, you'll train your meter to reject false things about him and pursue true things about him.

Bite, Don't Balk

The difference between working hard to understand and then apply principles about Jesus to your life, and pouring your energy into simply knowing Jesus better, is the difference between a description of what's in the center of an ice cream bar and actually biting into one. Here's the way of relating that Jesus modeled for us.

Rather than...

- describing what it's like to walk on water, he invites Peter to do it with him;

- helping the "rich young ruler" to understand the benefits of following him, Jesus simply asks him to sell everything he owns and start walking with him;

- telling his disciples all the reasons why they should offer mercy to others, he forgives the soldiers who are crucifying him.

- urging his followers to "love their enemies, and pray for those who persecute you," he accepts dinner invitations from his worst critics.

When Jesus entered Jerusalem on his way to the cross, and the people were worshipping him as the Messiah, the Pharisees demanded that this blasphemy stop. They were offended that Jesus was being hailed as a Savior, the Son of God. But Jesus responded: "If these become silent, the stones will cry out" (Luke 19:40). Our calling as followers of Jesus is to make sure those rocks stay silent, because we're the ones who are proclaiming the truth about him—his attributes, power, and nature. We do what he says to do, and we always tell the truth about him.

"DOING WHAT HE'S ASKED US TO DO." THIS LITTLE SENTENCE IS ACTUALLY A MASSIVE CHALLENGE, ISN'T IT? IT REQUIRES TWO THINGS THAT MOST PEOPLE WHO CLAIM TO BE FOLLOWERS OF JESUS RARELY DO.

FIRST, IT MEANS WE NEED TO KNOW WHAT IT IS JESUS IS ASKING US TO DO! THERE ARE SOME THINGS THAT HE WILL ASK YOU TO DO AT ANY GIVEN MOMENT. AND WE KNOW WHAT THOSE THINGS ARE BY TALKING TO HIM AND LISTENING TO THE HOLY SPIRIT AS WE GO THROUGH OUR DAY!

SECOND, AND THIS IS WHERE IT GETS TOUGH, WE NEED TO BE WILLING TO ACTUALLY DO WHAT WE KNOW HE WANTS US TO DO! HERE ARE SOME TIPS...

- WE KNOW FOR SURE JESUS WANTS US TO LOVE OUR ENEMIES. HOW ARE YOU DOING THAT?

- WE KNOW FOR SURE JESUS WANTS US TO OFFER UNLIMITED FORGIVENESS. WHO DO YOU NEED TO FORGIVE?

- WE KNOW FOR SURE THAT JESUS, THROUGH THE HOLY SPIRIT, IS NUDGING YOU TO DO SOMETHING TODAY. WILL YOU BE WILLING TO SAY YES?

"DOING WHAT HE'S ASKED US TO DO."
TRY IT, YOU'LL LIKE IT!

Pursuing Parables

Jesus taught, primarily, using parables. And in general, his parables can be divided into two basic "species"—the first kind describes the "norms" of the kingdom of God, and the second focuses on revealing the character and personality of God. You can use either species as a launching pad for knowing Jesus more intimately.

When you run across a parable, simply ask yourself one of these two questions: "What is this parable telling me about the kingdom of God?" or "What is this parable telling me about God's character or personality?" Here's a sampler list of parables that fit into both categories:

The kingdom of God is like...

Parable of Wheat and Weeds—Matthew 13:24-30 (God is more concerned about growing wheat than pulling weeds.)

Parable of the Pine Nut (or Mustard Seed)—Matthew 13:31-32 (What seems small can grow huge. Strength is nurtured over time.)

Parable of the Yeast—Matthew 13:33 (A small addition makes a big difference.) *Read story*

God is like...

Parable of the Moneylender—Luke 7:40-47 (He is an appreciator of the desperate and indebted.)

Parable of the Lost Sheep—Luke 15:3-7 (He is a pursuer of lost valuables; and he's a partier.)

Parable of the Lost Coin—Luke 15:8-10 (He is diligent, and he won't give up until he finds what he's looking for.)

I was lost

RE-FRAME-ABLE

ONE OF THE REASONS JESUS' PARABLES WERE SO EFFECTIVE WAS BECAUSE HE TOOK EVERYDAY THINGS OR COMMON-LIFE SITUATIONS AND USED THEM TO TEACH A POWERFUL TRUTH. HE WAS A GENIUS AT MAKING COMPLICATED THINGS EASY TO UNDERSTAND. UNFORTUNATELY MANY CHRISTIANS DO THE OPPOSITE; THEY MAKE FAIRLY SIMPLE TRUTHS ABOUT GOD HARD FOR OUTSIDERS TO UNDERSTAND! JESUS KNEW HIS AUDIENCE, AND HE KNEW WHAT TYPES OF STORIES AND ILLUSTRATIONS WOULD HELP THEM GRASP WHAT HE WAS TRYING TO COMMUNICATE-IT WAS AN INCREDIBLY EFFECTIVE METHOD!

THE MOMENT WILL COME (MAYBE SOMETIME SOON) WHERE YOU WILL HAVE A CHANCE TO EXPLAIN SOMETHING ABOUT GOD, JESUS, OR YOUR FAITH TO SOMEBODY WHO KNOWS VERY LITTLE ABOUT ANY OF THOSE THINGS. MAYBE, INSTEAD OF USING BIG, CHURCHY, WORDS OR OVERWHELMING THEM WITH TOO MANY SCRIPTURES, TRY JESUS' STRATEGY AND USE A STORY, AN OBJECT-A PARABLE OF YOUR OWN-TO HELP MAKE THE COMPLICATED A LITTLE EASIER FOR AN OUTSIDER TO UNDERSTAND.

My story goes like this...

Your True Name

If you were born a Native American 200 years ago, or a Jew 2,000 years ago, the name you received from your parents wouldn't merely express something that sounded nice, or be tied to a family name. Your name would've represented an identity your parents hoped you would live into. It would be less of a label and more of a hopeful description. That's because Jews and Native Americans understood something that's true in the kingdom of God: The names we embrace in our life are the names we become.

After the fisherman Simon "names" Jesus as Messiah, Jesus renames him Peter (Petros, which means "rock"). Jesus says, "I also say to you that you are Peter, and upon this rock I will build My church; and the gates of Hades will not overpower it" (Matthew 16:18). In renaming his closest friend with a descriptive word that had never before been used as a name, Jesus answers two big questions for him: "Who am I?" and "What am I doing here?" As we name Jesus, he names us. And the name he gives us projects onto us an identity born out of his faith in us. In the church we often talk about our faith in Jesus, but we rarely explore the biblical reality that Jesus has faith in us. He is bent on revealing our true identity.

As we pursue a grand adventure in our life—"Who do I say Jesus is?—we pursue a companion adventure at the same time—

"WHO DOES JESUS SAY I AM?"

JUST FOR FUN... KNOWING WHAT YOU KNOW TO BE TRUE ABOUT JESUS, AND KNOWING WHAT YOU KNOW ABOUT YOURSELF, IF HE WERE TO GIVE YOU A NICKNAME, WHAT DO YOU THINK IT WOULD BE? WHY? AND HOW WOULD THAT IMPACT THE WAY YOU SEE YOURSELF?

....

WE'RE ALMOST DONE! BUT WE WANT TO ASK YOU TO DO ONE LAST THING:

 PUT YOUR FINGER ON THIS PAGE AND FLIP BACK TO THE VERY FIRST CHAPTER. TAKE A LOOK AT THE THINGS ABOUT JESUS YOU WROTE DOWN IN YOUR PICTURE FRAME.

NOW THAT YOU'VE SPENT SOME TIME "REFRAMING" JESUS AS YOU READ THIS BOOK, IS THERE ANYTHING YOU'D CHANGE? IS THERE SOMETHING YOU'D ADD TO THE LIST?

WE HOPE THIS BOOK HAS HELPED YOU EXAMINE, UNDERSTAND, AND GET TO KNOW THE REAL JESUS BETTER. AND LIKE THE TITLE SAYS, WE HOPE IT HAS HELPED YOU "REFRAME" HIM. BUT THAT'S ONLY PART OF THE REASON WE WROTE THIS BOOK. IF WE'VE

ONLY SERVED TO HELP YOU REFRAME JESUS IN YOUR OWN MIND, WE'VE FAILED. OTHER PEOPLE-YOUR FRIENDS, YOUR NEIGHBORS, MAYBE EVEN YOUR YOUTH GROUP MEMBERS-NEED TO KNOW THE REAL JESUS, TOO!

HOLD UP YOUR RIGHT HAND (SERIOUSLY!) SO WE CAN DEPUTIZE YOU AS AN OFFICIAL "JESUS REFRAMER." READ THIS WITH YOUR HAND RAISED (SERIOUSLY):

"PEOPLE DESPERATELY NEEDS TO KNOW THE REAL JESUS, AND AS I SEEK TO KNOW HIM MORE AND MORE, HE WILL HELP ME REFRAME HOW THE WORLD SEES HIM. I AM TRUSTED AND EMPOWERED BY CHRIST TO REPRESENT HIM TO THOSE AROUND ME."

OK, YOU CAN PUT YOUR HAND DOWN NOW (SERIOUSLY!).

THE JESUS-CENTERED SUITE
FOR EVERY YOUTH MINISTRY!

JESUS-CENTERED SUITE
$39.99

INCLUDED IN THE SUITE:

1. Jesus-Centered Youth Ministry
2. Jesus-Centered Youth Ministry: Guide for Volunteers
3. Reframing Jesus DVD Curriculum
4. Reframing Jesus Devotional

simply youth ministry
helping youth workers with what matters most

GUIDE YOUR ENTIRE MINISTRY TO A JESUS-CENTERED FOCUS WITH THESE INNOVATIVE RESOURCES.

J.
JESUS-CENTERED

Guide your entire ministry toward a passionate Jesus-centered focus with this series of innovative resources. Harness the power of these dynamic tools that will help you draw teenagers and leaders into a closer orbit around Jesus.

SHIFT THE FOCUS OF YOUR MINISTRY

Jesus-Centered Youth Ministry
Moving From Jesus-Plus to Jesus-Only
By Rick Lawrence

DRAW YOUR TEAM CLOSER TO JESUS

Jesus-Centered Youth Ministry: Guide for Volunteers
Moving From Jesus-Plus to Jesus-Only
By Rick Lawrence

REINTRODUCE TEENAGERS TO THE REAL JESUS

Reframing Jesus DVD Curriculum
A Fresh Look Into a Familiar Face
4-Week Small Group Video Curriculum
By Kurt Johnston (with 6 Bonus Training Videos for Leaders by Rick Lawrence)

HELP STUDENTS LIVE A JESUS-CENTERED LIFE

Reframing Jesus Devotional
A Fresh Look Into a Familiar Face
By Rick Lawrence and Kurt Johnston;
Illustration by Storm

To learn more and purchase this essential suite for your ministry, go to

simplyyouthministry.com